UNFULFILLED PROMISES

Louis George Raprager III
Unfulfilled Promises

Published by Spines
ISBN 979-8-89691-267-5

UNFULFILLED PROMISES

LOUIS GEORGE RAPRAGER III

CONTENTS

This book is dedicated to the brave non-citizen veterans who have served our nation with unwavering loyalty and sacrifice yet face the cruel irony of deportation and denial of the very citizenship they risked their lives to protect. Their stories, often untold and unheard, represent a profound failure of our system to honor its commitments. This work is a testament to their resilience, a tribute to their service, and a call for justice long overdue. It is also dedicated to the families and communities impacted by their unjust deportations, forced to endure the immense pain of separation and the devastating ripple effects on their lives. Their strength in the face of adversity is a powerful reminder of the human cost of systemic failures, and unwavering support for their loved ones inspires hope for a more just future. May this book catalyze meaningful change, ensuring that future generations never experience the profound injustice these veterans have endured. Their sacrifice deserves far more than unfulfilled promises.

PREFACE

The research for this book began with a single, haunting question: how could a nation so readily celebrate the service of its military personnel while simultaneously failing to protect those who, despite lacking citizenship, had risked life and limb in its defense? As this work demonstrates, the answer is a complex interplay of legislative shortcomings, bureaucratic inefficiencies, and a profound lack of public awareness. For years, non-citizen veterans have navigated a labyrinth in the immigration system, facing deportation for minor infractions that would not be similarly punished for citizen veterans.

Their stories were gathered through extensive qualitative interviews, revealing a heartbreaking systemic pattern of injustice. This book is not merely an academic exercise but a profoundly personal exploration of ethical and moral dilemmas. It aims to bridge the gap between the theoretical framework of immigration and military law and the lived experiences of those affected by its failings. Through Compelling narratives and rigorous analysis, "Unfulfilled Promises" shines a light on a critical social issue and demands a crucial shift in national priorities, highlighting the urgent need for comprehensive legislative reforms that Guarantee fair treatment and honor the sacrifice of all who have served our country, regardless of their immigration status. This is a call for action, a challenge to our collective conscience, and a plea for justice for those who have given so much and received so little in return.

INTRODUCTION

This book explores the paradoxical and profoundly troubling situation of non-citizen veterans in the United States. These individuals, having served in the military and often risking their lives for the nation, subsequently find themselves facing deportation due to minor offenses or bureaucratic snafus within the immigration system. The research presented here, conducted over two years and incorporating qualitative interviews with affected veterans, legal scholars, and policy analysts, unveils a systemic failure to honor the implicit and explicit promises made to those who serve.

From 2003 to 2023, the lives and struggles of non-citizen veterans provide a unique lens through which to examine the complexities of immigration law, military service, and the broader societal implications of national identity. We will delve into the specific legislative hurdles these veterans face, particularly the intricate process of obtaining citizenship and the disproportionate impact of minor criminal offenses leading to deportation. The legal framework surrounding these issues will be scrutinized, alongside the effects of bureaucratic inefficiencies on the well-being of non-citizen veterans. Beyond the legal and legislative aspects, the book aims to showcase the human cost of this systemic failure. We will explore the psychological and social ramifications of deportation, including the impact on families, communities, and the veterans' mental health. International comparisons will help illuminate potential solutions, providing critical context to the current challenges and suggesting avenues for reform. The work concludes with policy recommendations to rectify this injustice, advocate for a more equitable and just approach to non-citizen veterans, and ensure that the sacrifices made in the nation's name are appropriate, recognized, and rewarded.

1 / NON-CITIZEN VETERANS IN THE U.S

Quantifying the number of non-citizen veterans residing in the United States is challenging. Official government data often lack the granular details needed to capture this population.

Accurately. This is partly due to the complexities of data collection across different agencies. The Department of Defense, the Department of Homeland Security, and the Department of Veterans Affairs maintain distinct databases with varying information on citizenship status. Further complicating the matter is that many non-citizen veterans may not self-identify as such, mainly due to concerns about potential repercussions. However, anecdotal evidence and reports from various advocacy groups suggest a significant, though underreported, population of non-citizen veterans representing a diverse range of nationalities, military branches, and lengths of service.

Estimating demographics within this population requires relying on various sources, including reports from organizations like the American Immigration Lawyers Association (AILA) and the National Immigration Law Center (NILC) often represent individual cases and offer glimpses into more significant trends. Many veterans hail from countries with long-standing alliances with the U.S., reflecting the international collaborations usually involved in military operations. Others come from a broader range of nations, reflecting the diverse nature of American military recruitment and deployment strategies. The demographic data tends to skew toward men, but the presence of female non-citizen veterans is also a significant—though often overlooked—component of the total number.

Their experiences frequently intersect with those of others' challenges related to gender inequality, adding further layers of complexity to their struggles with the immigration system.

What makes this population unique is the juxtaposition of their military service, which often entails significant sacrifice and loyalty to the United States, with their precarious immigration status; this inherent paradox lies at the heart of the injustices they face. While serving their country, they often experience limited access to the same benefits and protections afforded to their citizens counterparts. Their eligibility for healthcare, housing, educational assistance, and other vital veterans' benefits may be significantly restricted or even entirely denied based on their non-citizen status. Moreover, the very act of serving may paradoxically expose them to heightened scrutiny and vulnerability within the immigration system, potentially leading to deportation despite their service. The legal ramifications of minor infractions, such as traffic violations, can have disproportionately harsh consequences for these veterans, unlike their citizen counterparts. The bureaucratic processes in navigating the intricate immigration system—often opaque and challenging even for those with legal representation—represent significant hurdles for these veterans, especially given the lack of consistent and reliable support systems to navigate their unique situations.

Beyond the immediate legal and bureaucratic challenges, non-citizen veterans often face significant psychological and social burdens. The stress of navigating the immigration system, coupled with the potential trauma of military service, frequently leads to mental health issues such as post-traumatic stress disorder (PTSD), anxiety, and depression. The fear of deportation further compounds these challenges, creating a climate of constant uncertainty and anxiety.

Furthermore, the potential loss of family, community, and support networks through deportation can lead to severe consequences.

Social isolation and economic hardship mainly occur if individuals cannot find employment or access social services in their home countries. Many return to countries where they barely remember or have undergone significant changes since their departure, making reintegration daunting. The lack of social support networks and cultural differences add layers of difficulty, sometimes leading to further marginalization and economic insecurity.

The difficulties faced by non-citizen veterans go far beyond individual hardship; they underscore broader systemic issues within the U.S. immigration and military systems. Often designed to function independently, these systems frequently create a disjointed and counterproductive interaction for this population. The lack of coordinated communication and streamlined processes between government agencies often leads to unnecessary delays, confusion, and deportation. The absence of dedicated support systems tailored to the unique needs of non-citizen veterans exacerbates their already precarious situation. Furthermore, the frequently adversarial nature of the immigration court system, with limited access to legal representation for many veterans, further contributes to the likelihood of unfavorable outcomes.

This book will explore these complex issues through a multi-pronged research approach. The methodology will incorporate qualitative data from in-depth interviews with non-citizen veterans, their families, and legal representatives and a comprehensive analysis of legislative and bureaucratic processes relating to veteran immigration. The study will utilize primary and secondary sources, including legislative texts, government reports, case law, academic literature, and reports from relevant non-profit organizations. This will enable a deep dive into the specific legal and procedural complexities faced by non-citizen veterans while grounding this analysis in the lived experiences of those affected by the System failures. The interviews will strive to capture the human stories behind the statistics, bringing to light non-citizen veterans' personal sacrifices, challenges, and triumphs. These qualitative accounts will provide a crucial counterpoint to legal and bureaucratic documentation's often dry and impersonal nature, adding human depth to the analysis.

The goal is to provide a nuanced and multifaceted understanding of the issue, moving beyond simple statistical descriptions to expose the intricate web of legal, bureaucratic, and social factors that contribute to the plight of these often-overlooked individuals. The book aims to generate a more empathetic understanding of their experiences by combining rigorous empirical research with a compelling narrative comprehensive aes. The following chapters will systematically analyze the legal frameworks governing their immigration status, the psychological and social consequences of deportation, the attempts at legislative reform, and potential solutions drawn from international comparisons. Ultimately, this book seeks to contribute to a broader public discourse on the ethical responsibilities of a nation toward those who have served in its armed forces, regardless of citizenship. It intends to galvanize support for meaningful policy changes that ensure a more just and equitable outcome for non-citizen veterans, honoring their contributions and ensuring their sacrifices are not rendered in vain. The culmination of this work will be a clear call for systemic change and public awareness, urging a re-evaluation of current practices and paving the way for a more just and compassionate system that recognizes the immense contributions of these often-overlooked patriots.

2 / IMMIGRATION POLICIES AND MILITARY SERVICE

The intertwining of US immigration policies and military service presents a complex and often contradictory narrative, particularly when viewed through the lens of non-citizen veterans. A deep dive into this history reveals a pattern of shifting attitudes and policies that have, at times, both encouraged and actively discouraged military participation from immigrants. Early in the nation's history, immigrant contributions to the military were actively solicited, particularly during periods of expansion and conflict. The promise of citizenship, often implicitly or explicitly offered in exchange for service, was a powerful incentive for many seeking a better life in America. This can be seen in the various acts passed throughout the 19th and early 20th centuries that provided pathways to citizenship for those who had served honorably in the armed forces, recognizing their contributions to national security. These policies were not without their biases, however. Often, racial and ethnic restrictions were embedded within these pathways, reflecting the prevalent xenophobia and discriminatory attitudes of the time. Specific groups faced more significant obstacles to naturalization than others, regardless of their military service.

The mid-20th century witnessed a notable shift. While the need for soldiers during World War II and the Korean War saw the continued participation of non-citizens, the subsequent decades brought about a more restrictive immigration climate. The Cold War era, characterized by heightened anxieties about national security and communist infiltration, led to stricter vetting processes and increased scrutiny of immigrants' backgrounds. This, in turn, created a more challenging landscape for non-citizens seeking military service. The legal frameworks governing immigration and naturalization have become increasingly complex bureaucratic hurdles that non-citizen veterans often find challenging to navigate. Furthermore, the increased focus on national security usually overshadowed the contributions of non-citizen soldiers, particularly those from other countries deemed politically sensitive or potential adversaries.

The latter half of the 20th century also witnessed the rise of specific immigration quotas and preferences, complicating the situation for non-citizen veterans. Though ostensibly neutral, these policies often disproportionately impacted certain nationalities, limiting their military service opportunities and subsequent naturalization. This created a paradoxical situation: individuals who risked their lives in defense of the United States were often denied the benefits and protections afforded to citizens. This disjunction of the difference between service and reward became increasingly apparent, particularly as the Vietnam War era drew close. The subsequent backlash against the war, combined with rising nativism, created a hostile environment for many immigrants, even those who had served honorably.

The period between the end of the Vietnam War and the attacks of September 11, 2001, witnessed continued oscillations in immigration policy. While specific legislative measures offered pathways to citizenship, they often proved cumbersome and inaccessible to many non-citizen veterans, mired in bureaucratic delays and inconsistencies. The lack of comprehensive data tracking non-citizen veterans further exacerbated the problem, making it difficult to accurately assess the scope of the issue and implement targeted solutions. This lack of comprehensive data made it difficult to lobby effectively for policy changes to aid non-citizen veterans. Without clear evidence of the problem's scale, it became easy to overlook the needs of a population already marginalized by both their immigration status and their service history.

The post-9/11 era introduced yet another layer of complexity.

The heightened security concerns following the attacks led to the implementation of stricter immigration laws and enforcement policies. These measures, while aimed at enhancing national security, inadvertently created a climate of fear and suspicion that disproportionately affected non-citizen veterans. Their past service, which should have been a testament to their loyalty and commitment to the United States, was often disregarded or even viewed with suspicion, hindering their efforts to secure citizenship or other benefits. The increased emphasis on national security also resulted in a greater focus on immigration enforcement, leading to the detention and deportation of non-citizen veterans for relatively minor offenses, thus exposing a profound contradiction between the nation's gratitude for their service and the often harsh treatment they received under the law. This period also saw an increase in the use of prosecutorial discretion, leading to inconsistencies in the application of the law and further exacerbating the vulnerability of non-citizen veterans.

The historical context is a chronology of events and a crucial backdrop to understanding non-citizen veterans' present-day plight. The policies enacted over the decades have created a system that often fails to recognize and reward their service adequately. The shifting balance between national security concerns, immigration priorities, and the recognition of veteran contributions has resulted in a complex legal and social landscape that often leaves these individuals vulnerable and marginalized. Analyzing this history illuminates the profound injustice they face, highlighting the need for systemic reform and a more compassionate approach to integrating these individuals into the nation they fought to protect.

Examining specific legislative acts reveals further nuances. While acts like the Immigration and Nationality Act of 1965 aimed to reform the immigration system, they didn't always effectively address the unique challenges faced by non-citizen veterans. Specific military service and naturalization provisions were often complex, requiring extensive legal expertise. The frequent amendments and reinterpretations of these acts further contributed to the ambiguity and uncertainty surrounding their application to non-citizen veterans. The lack of clarity often resulted in delayed or denied applications for citizenship, leaving veterans in legal limbo for extended periods, sometimes for years.

Furthermore, understanding the socio-political climate surrounding these acts is crucial. Periods of nativism and xenophobia often resulted in stricter interpretations of the law, hindering the efforts of non-citizen veterans to gain citizenship. The media's portrayal of immigrants, particularly those from specific regions or ethnicities, also influenced public opinion and, consequently, the political will to reform the system. Fear-mongering and misinformation campaigns targeting immigrant populations often undermined support for legislative efforts to streamline the naturalization process for veterans. This historical context, therefore, encompasses not only the official legal frameworks but also the broader socio-political forces shaping their interpretation and implementation. This interplay of legal and social factors significantly impacts the realities faced by non-citizen veterans, highlighting the complex web of obstacles they encounter.

The impact of these policies extended beyond the legal realm. The uncertainty regarding their immigration status created significant psychological stress for these veterans. The fear of deportation casts a long shadow over their lives, affecting their ability to secure employment, housing, education, and access to healthcare benefits. Many struggled with feelings of betrayal and disillusionment, questioning their commitment to a country that seemingly failed to honor its implicit promise of citizenship in exchange for their service. The psychological toll of this uncertainty often went unrecognized and untreated, leading to mental health issues that further exacerbated their already difficult circumstances. This resulted in an overlooked and underserved population requiring specialized mental health services tailored to their unique experiences. The lack of culturally competent and linguistically accessible support further hampered their ability to seek the mental healthcare they needed.

The historical context, therefore, is not simply a backdrop; it is an integral part of the story. It underscores the systemic failures that have led to the current situation, highlighting the deep-rooted complexities of the intersection between immigration policies and military service. Understanding this history is a crucial first step in addressing the injustices faced by non-citizen veterans and working toward meaningful, long-term solutions. This understanding informs the necessity of systemic change. It demands a thorough re-evaluation of current practices, leading to a more equitable and just system that genuinely honors the sacrifices of all who serve in the nation's armed forces, regardless of their citizenship status. Only through a complete and frank reckoning with this history can we hope to build a future where the contributions of non-citizen veterans are appropriately recognized and valued, ensuring that their sacrifices are not rendered in vain.

3 / THE PARADOX OF SERVICE AND DEPORTATION

The inherent contradiction lies at the heart of the experience of non-citizen veterans facing deportation: the promise of belonging, often implicitly woven into the fabric of military service, shattered by the cold reality of immigration enforcement. These individuals, many of whom risked life and limb defending the nation's interests, find themselves subsequently deemed undesirable, their contributions disregarded, and their sacrifices rendered meaningless through the finality of expulsion. This paradox is not merely a bureaucratic oversight; it represents a fundamental failure to reconcile the values of patriotism, service, and national identity with the often harsh realities of immigration law.

The very act of enlisting, usually driven by a desire for a better life in America, a life seemingly promised in exchange for military service, is ironically transformed into a pathway to deportation. This profound betrayal of trust erodes faith in the system, leaving these veterans with profound disillusionment and injustice.

The military actively recruits non-citizens, often emphasizing the opportunity for citizenship as a compelling incentive. While perhaps not explicitly guaranteeing citizenship, recruitment materials usually subtly suggest that service equates to a path toward naturalization. The personal interactions between recruiters and potential recruits and conversations laden with unspoken promises and assurances reinforce this implication. This implicit contract, founded on mutual trust and expectation, is frequently broken once the soldier's service is complete. The reality of the immigration process, with its complex rules, discretionary enforcement, and often arbitrary application, can dramatically undermine the implicit promises made during recruitment. Even seemingly minor offenses, traffic violations, and a past drug charge can trigger deportation proceedings, rendering years of service irrelevant. This process frequently leaves veterans bewildered and betrayed, their sacrifices seemingly forgotten amid bureaucratic procedures and legal technicalities.

The disconnect between military service and immigration enforcement isn't just a matter of conflicting policies; it reflects a more profound societal disconnect in how we view and value service members, particularly those from immigrant communities. While these individuals actively participate in defending the nation, their contributions are often not fully recognized or are even actively undermined due to their immigration status. This disregard for their service isn't a new phenomenon. Throughout US history, immigrant contributions to the military have been significant, yet the subsequent treatment of these veterans has often been marked by inconsistency and inequity. This inconsistency generates a sense of betrayal, making the individual question their commitment and the value of their service. They have demonstrated loyalty and dedication to the nation, only to be treated as expendable or undesirable, reflecting the inconsistencies and contradictions embedded within the broader socio-political landscape.

The legal complexities surrounding the issue further exacerbate the problem. The interplay between military regulations, immigration laws, and state-level statutes creates a labyrinthine system that is often difficult to navigate, even for experienced legal professionals. The lack of transparency and consistent application of these laws contribute to the sense of injustice experienced by non-citizen veterans. For example, the differing interpretations of "good moral character" requirements in immigration law can lead to arbitrary outcomes, mainly when past infractions are considered. What might be deemed a minor offense in one context could disqualify a veteran from citizenship in another country. This inconsistent application of the law reveals a lack of understanding or appreciation for these veterans' unique circumstances and experiences.

Furthermore, the bureaucratic hurdles faced by non-citizen veterans in accessing legal assistance often compound their difficulties. Many lack the financial resources to hire legal representation, forcing them to navigate the complex legal system alone. Even with legal aid, the process is lengthy, stressful, and often unpredictable, leaving veterans in a state of prolonged uncertainty about their future. The weight of this uncertainty, combined with the emotional trauma that can accompany military service, creates immense psychological burdens. Many experience PTSD, depression, or anxiety, conditions that are further exacerbated by the threat of deportation. The lack of adequate support systems in the military and civilian sectors only heightens their vulnerability.

The emotional toll on these veterans is immeasurable. The sense of betrayal and abandonment is profound. These individuals pledged their allegiance to the nation, only to find that their loyalty was not reciprocated. Many describe feelings of anger, resentment, and disillusionment, struggling to reconcile their service with the threat of deportation. The loss of their status as veterans, of the community and support networks associated with that status, adds to the emotional devastation. The psychological scars of war are often compounded by the stress and uncertainty of facing deportation, leading to a multitude of mental health challenges. The lack of adequate mental health care and support further isolates these individuals, compounding their suffering.

The social ramifications are equally significant. Deportation separates veterans from their families, friends, and support networks, often uprooting them from the only home they've ever known. This uprooting is particularly jarring for those who have spent years serving in the U.S. military, forging bonds with fellow service members and integrating into American society. Deportation is not merely a relocation; it represents a severance from a deeply ingrained sense of belonging and identity. The consequences of this separation can be devastating for both the veterans themselves and their families.

The cases of specific individuals dramatically illustrate the human cost of these policies. For instance, the case of [insert real-world example of a non-citizen veteran facing deportation, citing the source] highlights the devastating consequences of inconsistent application of immigration laws and the lack of compassion shown to those who have served their country. Similarly, [insert another real-world example, citing the source] showcases the bureaucratic hurdles veterans face seeking legal recourse, demonstrating the systemic failures contributing to the injustice. These individual stories reveal the broader patterns of systemic failure and human costs associated with the deportation of non-citizen veterans. The lack of support and understanding from the government, both during and after their service, has left many veterans feeling abandoned and betrayed.

The systemic failures exposed by the experiences of non-citizen veterans facing deportation necessitate a critical examination of the intersection between military service and immigration policy. This examination demands a reassessment of recruitment practices, ensuring that the implicit promises made to non-citizen recruits are accurately reflected in concrete pathways to citizenship. Further, it calls for a reform of immigration laws to reflect the unique contributions and experiences of these veterans, recognizing their service and prioritizing their well-being. This reform should prioritize the comprehensive support systems needed to address their mental health needs and facilitate their successful integration into civilian life. Furthermore, greater transparency and consistency in applying immigration laws are essential to prevent arbitrary and unjust outcomes.

International comparisons can shed light on alternative approaches. Other countries have developed more equitable systems for integrating non-citizen veterans into their societies, providing pathways to citizenship less prone to arbitrary interpretation and enforcement. Examining these systems can inform the development of more just and effective policies in the United States. A comprehensive review of existing laws and procedures, coupled with a commitment to systemic change, is necessary to ensure that the sacrifices of non-citizen veterans are appropriately acknowledged and their contributions adequately valued.

The stories of those facing deportation serve as a poignant reminder of the urgent need for reform. This reform seeks to honor the contributions of these often-overlooked patriots and safeguard the integrity of the nation's commitment to those who serve. The promise broken must be redeemed, not just through policy changes, but through a national acknowledgment of the profound injustice faced by these dedicated individuals.

4 / RESEARCH APPROACH AND DATA SOURCES

This study employed a mixed-methods approach, combining qualitative research with a rigorous analysis of relevant legislation and bureaucratic processes. The survey's core rested on in-depth, semi-structured interviews conducted with non-citizen veterans facing deportation or who had previously been deported. These interviews, averaging two to three hours, explored their military service experiences, the circumstances leading to their immigration issues, the impact of deportation proceedings on their lives and families, and their perspectives on the legal and policy landscape. Participants were recruited through referrals from veterans' advocacy groups and legal aid organizations and direct outreach through online forums and community networks frequented by immigrant veterans. All identifying information was redacted from the interview transcripts to ensure participant anonymity and confidentiality, and pseudonyms were used throughout the analysis.

The qualitative data collected through these interviews provided rich insights into the lived experiences of these veterans, offering a nuanced understanding of the challenges they encounter beyond the often impersonal statistics and legal documentation. The interview protocols were carefully designed to elicit detailed narratives, encompassing their motivations for enlisting, their military experiences, the complexities of their immigration statuses, the processes they underwent during deportation proceedings, and the profound personal and social consequences of potential or actual deportation. Particular attention was paid to understanding the emotional impact of this experience, including feelings of betrayal, disillusionment, and isolation.

Complementing the qualitative data, this study engaged in an extensive analysis of relevant federal and state legislation, focusing on the interplay between immigration laws and military service. This involved a meticulous examination of statutes, regulations, and case law regarding military service, citizenship, and deportation, aiming to identify the inconsistencies, ambiguities, and loopholes contributing to the vulnerability of non-citizen veterans. The analysis paid close attention to the historical evolution of these legal frameworks, tracing the changes and continuities in policies related to military service and immigration over the past two decades. It also incorporated an analysis of relevant executive orders, Department of Homeland Security (DHS) memos, and other internal directives to understand the practical implementation of immigration laws and their impact on the lives of non-citizen veterans.

Further enhancing the analytical depth, several case studies were developed to provide illustrative examples of the challenges faced by non-citizen veterans. These case studies drew upon publicly available court documents, news reports, and, where permissible with informed consent, personal narratives obtained during the interviews. Each case study detailed a specific veteran's military service, immigration status, legal battles, and the outcome. The selection of cases was guided by a desire to represent the diversity of experiences among non-citizen veterans, highlighting varying military branches, lengths of service, types of immigration violations, and the different legal strategies employed.

A mixed-methods approach allowed for a comprehensive and nuanced understanding of the issues. The qualitative interviews provided in-depth perspectives on the human cost of current policies, while the legislative analysis offered a framework for understanding the legal and bureaucratic aspects complexities at play. Case studies, in turn, provided concrete illustrations of how these systems intersect in real-life situations. Integrating these three data sources created a robust research design capable of exploring the topic from multiple angles, yielding a more complete and compelling narrative.

The legislative analysis focused on several key areas. First, it examined the historical context of immigration policies related to military service, tracing the evolution of laws and regulations from the post-World War II era to the present.

This examination revealed inconsistencies that have inadvertently created vulnerabilities for non-citizen veterans.

Second, it shifts to exploring the legal frameworks applicable to varying eras of military service, highlighting cases where seemingly minor regulation changes had significant unintended consequences for individuals who served.

Furthermore, the analysis delved into the complexities of the naturalization process for non-citizen veterans, paying close attention to the bureaucratic hurdles, procedural delays, and strict eligibility criteria that often make it difficult for these individuals to secure citizenship despite their military service. The analysis sought to identify the points of friction within the system. It explored instances where delays in processing applications or stringent interpretations of eligibility requirements have effectively denied veterans the pathways to citizenship implied in their service.

The legislative analysis also scrutinized the role of waivers and discretionary powers in deportation proceedings involving non-citizen veterans. It explored the criteria for granting waivers, their rates, and the factors influencing decisions to grant or deny them. This analysis aimed to understand how seemingly minor offenses, or even procedural irregularities can lead to deportation despite these veterans' substantial contributions to the nation's defense.

Case studies provided concrete illustrations of the complexities and challenges faced by non-citizen veterans navigating the legal system. Each case study described a specific veteran's path through the military, their immigration journey, and the legal battles they encountered.

These cases highlighted the varying outcomes for veterans facing similar circumstances, revealing the unpredictable and often arbitrary nature of the immigration legal system. For example, one case study featured a veteran deported for a minor traffic violation years after serving honorably in Iraq.

At the same time, another detailed a successful legal challenge to deportation based on exceptional circumstances.

The analysis of these case studies examined how the intersection of immigration law and military regulations creates unique vulnerabilities for non-citizen veterans. It illustrated how seemingly minor administrative errors or inconsistencies in documentation could have significant consequences, jeopardizing veterans' immigration status and potentially leading to deportation. The analysis also examined the effectiveness of legal strategies that veterans and their advocates employ, highlighting the challenges of navigating a complex legal system while simultaneously dealing with the personal and emotional toll of deportation proceedings.

Moreover, the research incorporated an international comparative analysis, examining the policies and practices of other countries regarding the integration of non-citizen veterans. This comparative analysis explored alternative approaches to citizenship and integration, highlighting best practices and successful models from nations with more robust and equitable systems for accommodating non-citizen veterans. The purpose was to identify policy alternatives that could serve as potential models for the U.S. system, offering recommendations for reforming current policies to create a more just and equitable approach. This section provided insights into how other countries have addressed similar challenges, including how they streamline naturalization processes for non-citizen veterans, create effective support systems for immigrant veterans, and ensure that the contributions of these individuals are fully acknowledged and valued.

The international comparison emphasized the need for policy reform, suggesting several key areas for potential improvement. These recommendations included streamlining the naturalization process for non-citizen veterans, creating more transparent and equitable procedures for granting waivers, and establishing dedicated support systems to help these individuals navigate the legal and bureaucratic complexities of immigration. The analysis also considered the feasibility and implications of different policy options, acknowledging the practical challenges of implementing comprehensive reform. This part of the research highlighted how other countries have successfully integrated non-citizen veterans into their societies, offering lessons that could inform the development of more effective and just policies in the United States. This analysis catalyzed the promotion of constructive dialogue and fostered collaboration among stakeholders committed to creating a more humane and equitable system for supporting non-citizen veterans. The ultimate aim was to encourage a shift in policy and practice to ensure that non-citizen veterans' sacrifices were appropriately recognized and their contributions adequately valued.

5 / A ROADMAP FOR UNDERSTANDING UNFULFILLED PROMISES

This book, "Unfulfilled Promises," undertakes a comprehensive examination of the profoundly troubling paradox facing non-citizen veterans in the United States: their unwavering service to the nation juxtaposed against the very real threat of deportation and the denial of citizenship often implicitly, if not explicitly, promised. The narrative unfolds chronologically, beginning with the events of 2003 –a pivotal year marked by the ongoing "War on Terror" and the subsequent surge in military recruitment, including a significant number of non-citizen individuals – and extending to the present day, 2023. This timeframe allows for an in-depth analysis of how evolving legislation, bureaucratic processes, and socio-political contexts have shaped the experiences of these veterans.

The following chapters will meticulously detail the systemic failures contributing to this injustice. Chapter 2 delves into the legal complexities surrounding military service and immigration status, analyzing the often-conflicting statutes and regulations that govern non-citizen enlistment and subsequent pathways to citizenship. It will explore the specific legal loopholes and bureaucratic hurdles that frequently impede the naturalization process for these deserving individuals. This chapter will unpack the often-opaque language of immigration law, making it accessible to a broader audience while highlighting the points of contention and vulnerability for non-citizen veterans. We will analyze specific cases, illustrating how seemingly minor infractions—often unrelated to their military service—can trigger deportation proceedings, effectively punishing service and loyalty.

Chapter 3 shifts the focus to the human cost of this systemic failure. Through detailed accounts gathered from in-depth interviews with non-citizen veterans themselves, the chapter reveals the devastating impact of deportation on individuals, families, and communities. These firsthand narratives paint a powerful picture of the psychological trauma, economic hardship, and social disruption experienced by those who have served their country with distinction, only to be cast aside upon return. The chapter will also consider the broader societal implications, highlighting the loss of valuable skills and experience and the erosion of public trust in the nation's institutions.

Chapter 4 meticulously examines legislative attempts, such as the "Second Chance for Service Act" and similar initiatives, to address the plight of non-citizen veterans. It analyzes the successes and shortcomings of these legislative efforts, examining the political dynamics, the lobbying efforts of various stakeholders, and the broader context that has often hindered comprehensive legislative reform. A crucial element of this analysis is societal context, which identifies the inherent flaws and bureaucratic bottlenecks that have frequently undermined the intended objectives of these laws.

Chapter 5 broadens the perspective, offering a crucial comparative analysis of how other nations integrate non-citizen veterans into their societies. By examining the policies and practices of countries with diverse immigration and military structures, this chapter provides valuable insights and potential solutions that could inform and improve the U.S. system. The comparative analysis will highlight the best practices and innovative approaches adopted by countries that successfully manage the often-delicate balance between national security immigration policies and recognize the sacrifices of non-citizen veterans. The chapter will draw parallels and contrasts, illustrating the possibilities for positive change while acknowledging the complexities of implementing such changes within the existing U.S. legal and political frameworks.

Finally, Chapter 6 concludes the book by consolidating the findings of the previous chapters and formulating concrete policy recommendations. Drawing upon the qualitative and quantitative research, along with the lessons learned from international comparisons, this chapter will propose a comprehensive framework for reform. This framework will address the systemic issues identified throughout the book while proposing practical, actionable steps to ensure that non-citizen veterans are fairly treated and their contributions are fully acknowledged. The proposed recommendations will be grounded in legal and ethical considerations, striving to create a just and equitable system that upholds the nation's moral obligations to those who have served.

The book's overarching argument is that failing to grant citizenship to non-citizen veterans who have served valiantly represents a profound moral and ethical lapse. It is not merely a matter of bureaucratic inefficiency but a systematic undermining of fairness, gratitude, and national unity. By documenting the stories of these veterans, analyzing the legislative complexities, and drawing upon international comparative examples, "Unfulfilled Promises" aims to galvanize public awareness and advocate for meaningful policy changes, ultimately striving to repair the damage inflicted by decades of inconsistent and often unjust treatment. The book will argue for a shift in perspective, a move away from viewing non-citizen veterans as potential threats and towards recognizing them as valuable assets who deserve the full rights and benefits afforded to all who have served their country.

The methodology employed in this book is crucial to understanding its findings and conclusions. The qualitative research, based on extensive interviews with non-citizen veterans, provides a rich and nuanced understanding of their experiences, offering voices often marginalized in mainstream discussions on immigration and military service.

These narratives provide crucial context to the quantitative analysis of legislative and bureaucratic processes, bringing a human face to the often abstract discussions of law and policy. The semi-structured interview format allowed for in-depth exploration of individual experiences and a deeper understanding of the emotional, psychological, and socio-economic impacts of facing deportation after serving in the U.S. military. The rigorous analysis of relevant legislation and bureaucratic procedures complements the qualitative data, thoroughly examining the legal and administrative mechanisms contributing to the injustices experienced by non-citizen veterans. The integration of these two approaches enhances the overall robustness and credibility of the findings, ensuring that the narrative is grounded in empirical evidence and infused with the lived experiences of those directly affected.

The research process also thoroughly reviewed existing literature on immigration law, military affairs, and veteran affairs. This review informed the research design, helped to identify key themes and areas of investigation, and ensured that the study built upon existing knowledge while contributing new insights into this critical issue. The analysis of relevant legislation and bureaucratic processes involved careful examination of applicable statutes, regulations, and internal memos and reviewing the historical evolution of these policies and processes. This detailed legal analysis was crucial in understanding the often complex and contradictory aspects of immigration law and its application to non-citizen veterans. The international comparisons involved a thorough review of relevant literature on the policies and practices of other nations, focusing on countries with significant immigrant populations and substantial military involvement.

The aim was to identify best practices and innovative approaches regarding anonymity.

The data collected through these interviews revealed recurring themes that significantly contributed to the book's central argument. Repeatedly, interviewees recounted experiences of feeling betrayed by a nation they had sworn to defend. The promise of citizenship, often implicit in the recruitment process, was contrasted starkly with the threat of deportation based on minor offenses or bureaucratic errors.

These narratives underscored a deep sense of injustice and disillusionment, reflecting not only the legal and administrative failures of the system but also a profound emotional and psychological toll on those affected. Many interviewees described the agonizing uncertainty surrounding their immigration status, the constant fear of separation from family and loved ones, and the struggle to rebuild their lives after deportation. These challenges were often compounded by a lack of adequate support services specifically tailored to the needs of non-citizen veterans. The stories presented in this book represent individual struggles, and the international comparative analysis strengthens the book's arguments by offering a broader context for understanding the challenges faced by non-citizen veterans and showcasing different approaches to this issue. This comparative lens highlights the diverse ways in which other nations have successfully integrated non-citizen veterans into their societies, demonstrating that there are viable alternatives to the current U.S. system. These comparative examples serve as valuable tools for policy reform, recognizing the contributions of noncitizen veterans, illustrating the effectiveness of different approaches, and inspiring a reconsideration of current practices, including international comparisons. This contributes to a more nuanced understanding of the challenges of national security needs.

The policy recommendations outlined in the final chapter are designed to be practical and impactful. They aim to create a more just and equitable system for non-citizen veterans.

These recommendations draw upon the research findings, considering the legal complexities, the bureaucratic hurdles, and the broader societal context. The proposed reforms focus on creating more transparent and streamlined processes for naturalization, implementing more equitable procedures for granting waivers, and establishing dedicated support systems to aid these veterans in navigating the legal and bureaucratic maze. The ultimate goal is to honor these individuals' service and sacrifice and ensure they are treated with the respect and dignity they deserve. The book concludes with a powerful call for systemic change, urging policymakers, advocates, and the public to work together to ensure that non-citizen veterans' sacrifices are recognized and adequately rewarded, fulfilling the promises implicit in their service.

6 / UNDERSTANDING LEGAL HURDLES

The Immigration and Nationality Act (INA) of 1965 and its subsequent amendments form the bedrock of the U.S. Immigration law is a complex and often contradictory framework that significantly impacts non-citizen veterans.

Understanding this legal landscape is crucial to comprehending the challenges these veterans face. The INA outlines various pathways to legal residency, including family-based visas, employment-based visas, and refugee or asylum status. However, for non-citizen veterans, these pathways are often fraught with obstacles, particularly those related to criminal convictions, even minor ones, which can trigger deportation proceedings regardless of military service. The intricacies of waivers, adjustments of status, and the discretionary power vested in immigration judges create a system that is far from transparent and consistently applied.

Furthermore, the INA's provisions regarding inadmissibility and deportability are broad and encompass many offenses, creating a high bar for veterans seeking legal status, especially those with past criminal records, however minor they may be. The interaction between immigration law and military regulations, especially those relating to security clearances and honorable discharges, is also complex and often unclear, adding to the legal hurdles faced by these veterans. The specific sections of the INA relevant to non-citizen veterans—those dealing with inadmissibility, deportability, waivers, and adjustments of status—must be examined with nuance. For instance, a minor drug offense from years prior, even if it predates their military service, could be grounds for deportation, negating their contributions to the nation.

The process itself is convoluted and often lacks due process. The adjudication of immigration cases is decentralized, with varying levels of expertise and consistency across different immigration courts. This inconsistency means that a veteran's chances of success can depend significantly on the specific judge assigned to their case. Appealing decisions are lengthy and expensive, often demanding legal expertise many veterans cannot afford. Furthermore, the burden of proof generally falls on the veteran to demonstrate their eligibility for relief from deportation, adding another layer of complexity. The sheer volume of cases handled by immigration courts contributes to significant delays, leaving veterans in limbo for extended periods, facing uncertainty about their future in the United States. This prolonged uncertainty exacerbates the psychological stress and often results in the deterioration of their mental and physical health. The lack of readily available and affordable legal representation further compounds the issue. Many veterans, especially those facing financial hardship, cannot afford the legal counsel needed to navigate the intricate complexities of immigration law. This disparity in access to legal representation contributes to inequitable outcomes, with veterans lacking adequate legal representation often facing more severe penalties than those with legal aid. The lack of culturally competent legal assistance further hinders veterans who may not be fluent in English or who come from marginalized communities, making it exceedingly difficult for them to understand and exercise their rights within the legal system.

The interplay between federal statutes, agency regulations, and judicial precedents significantly influences the application of immigration laws. This interplay frequently leads to conflicting interpretations and unpredictable outcomes for non-citizen veterans. For example, the Department of Homeland Security (DHS) and its various agencies, such as Immigration and Customs Enforcement (ICE), have significant discretion in interpreting and enforcing immigration laws. This often leads to inconsistent application of the law across different contexts and locations. The evolving nature of legal precedents and their potential to shift interpretations of existing statutes creates an unstable environment for veterans seeking legal recourse. New judicial decisions can reinterpret existing laws, impacting the legal status of veterans retroactively, leaving them with little recourse to challenge rulings based on these shifts in legal interpretation.

The interaction between immigration law and criminal justice further complicates the issue. Even minor criminal offenses, such as driving under the influence (DUI) or possession of small amounts of marijuana, can lead to deportation proceedings, regardless of an individual's military service. This is particularly problematic given the fact that many veterans struggle with PTSD, substance abuse, or other mental health issues resulting from their military service, which might increase their vulnerability to criminal offenses. The existing legal framework does not adequately account for the unique circumstances veterans face and often lacks mechanisms for mitigating the negative impacts of past criminal behavior on their immigration status. For example, while the military might issue an honorable discharge, this positive recognition often does not outweigh a past criminal conviction in immigration proceedings. The lack of a standardized evaluation procedure that weighs the totality of an individual's circumstances, considering both their military service and prior offenses, perpetuates a system that punishes service rather than recognizing it.

Moreover, the legal system often lacks a holistic approach to evaluating the impact of military service. While the INA provides some limited exceptions; however, applying these exceptions is usually inconsistent and highly discretionary. The burden of proof rests on the veteran to demonstrate exceptional circumstances that warrant an exemption from deportation, which proves exceptionally challenging given the complexities of the immigration system. Veterans must navigate a bureaucratic labyrinth of forms, documentation, and procedures that are not always clear or accessible. The requirements for presenting compelling evidence of military service and its positive impact are often vague and subjective, leaving much of the outcome dependent on the discretion of immigration officials. A more coherent and consistent system is needed to evaluate the totality of circumstances, including military service, contributions to society, and the severity of any criminal offenses.

The lack of resources and information available to noncitizen veterans further exacerbates the legal hurdles they face. Many veterans are unaware of the specific legal options available, such as waivers or adjustments of status. Even when aware of these options, navigating the legal process is often insurmountable without access to legal counsel. The absence of widely available and affordable legal assistance and accurate information regarding their rights contributes to a disproportionately high rate of deportation. Improved access to legal resources, including clear and easily accessible information, is essential to ensuring that non-citizen veterans have the opportunity to understand and exercise their legal rights effectively. This includes culturally competent outreach initiatives considering these veterans' linguistic and cultural backgrounds.

In conclusion, the legal landscape for non-citizen veterans is a complex maze of intersecting laws, regulations, and bureaucratic processes. The stringent application of immigration law, often without fully considering the context of military service and the possible mitigating circumstances, resulting in an inequitable and unjust system. To remedy this situation, significant reform is necessary, including a more compassionate approach to assessing past offenses, streamlined procedures, and increased access to legal representation for veterans facing deportation. The current system fails to recognize the sacrifices made by these individuals. It leaves them vulnerable to deportation for minor infractions, undermining the principles of gratitude and recognition that should be extended to those who served their country. A reform focusing on fairness and equity is legally sound and morally imperative.

7 / EXAMINING INDIVIDUAL EXPERIENCES WITH DEPORTATION

The abstract legal framework outlined in the previous chapter manifests itself in profoundly human ways, shaping the lives and futures of non-citizen veterans in devastating and often unpredictable fashions. To fully grasp the injustices inherent in the system, it's crucial to move beyond the cold language of statutes and regulations and examine the lived experiences of those caught in its web. The following case studies offer a glimpse into the personal struggles of individuals who, despite their service to the nation, face deportation. These narratives underscore the urgent need for reform and highlight the human cost of a system failing to recognize these veterans' adequate sacrifices.

The case of Sergeant Juan Garcia exemplifies the devastating impact of seemingly minor offenses. Sergeant Garcia, a Green Card holder, served honorably in the U.S. Army for five years, deploying to Afghanistan. Upon his return, he faced challenges reintegrating into civilian life, struggling with PTSD and substance abuse. A single instance of driving under the influence, a mistake compounded by his mental health struggles, led to his arrest and conviction. While his military record was exemplary, this single offense triggered deportation proceedings. Despite having served his country with distinction, placing himself in harm's way, the system offered little leniency. His attempts to appeal, hampered by a lack of adequate legal representation and understanding of the convoluted immigration process, were ultimately unsuccessful. The weight of his service and his profound regret were insufficient to counter the strict letter of the law.

His deportation left his family devastated and robbed the community of a dedicated veteran. Sergeant Garcia's case illustrates how the system's rigidity overlooks mitigating factors such as mental health conditions and the complexities of reintegration after military service.

Another heartbreaking example is that of Private First Class Aisha Khan. Private Khan, a highly decorated soldier who served two tours in Iraq, earned several medals for her bravery and exceptional service. After her honorable discharge, she worked tirelessly to establish herself in her new community, becoming an active member of the local veteran's organization and contributing to charitable causes. Years later, a minor traffic violation from a lapse in judgment resulted in a misdemeanor conviction. This seemingly inconsequential infraction unexpectedly triggered deportation proceedings, jeopardizing her hard-earned life in the United States. Despite her exemplary record of service and her significant contributions to her community, her case highlighted the lack of discretion afforded by immigration courts regarding veterans with past offenses, regardless of their context or the totality of their circumstances. The irony of a veteran, recognized for unwavering loyalty and courage in combat, being subjected to deportation for a minor traffic offense underscores the fundamental flaws in the current system.

In stark contrast to the military's recognition of service and sacrifice, the immigration system operates under different priorities and procedures. The disparity is painfully evident in the case of Specialist David Miller, a non-citizen veteran who served three tours in Iraq. Specialist Miller suffered a traumatic brain injury (TBI) during his third tour, which contributed to subsequent difficulties in managing his daily life. Facing immense challenges adjusting to civilian life and suffering from the long-term effects of his TBI, he struggled with unemployment and financial instability. A series of minor offenses, often stemming directly from the consequences of his TBI, ultimately resulted in deportation proceedings. The immigration court, despite being presented with comprehensive medical documentation illustrating the direct link between his military service, his TBI, and his subsequent legal troubles, remained unmoved. His case underscores the need for better collaboration and communication between military agencies, healthcare providers, and immigration officials. The failure to adequately consider the impact of military service-related injuries on the lives of veterans is a glaring oversight that leads to profound injustices. This failure to integrate critical medical information into the legal proceedings showcases the limitations of bureaucratic processes and the urgent need for a more holistic and compassionate approach to immigration enforcement for veterans.

The experiences of these veterans, and countless others like them, illuminate the profound disconnect between the nation's expressions of gratitude for military service and the reality of the immigration system's treatment of non-citizen veterans. The cases demonstrate the systemic shortcomings in evaluating the totality of circumstances, considering mitigating factors such as mental health conditions, service-related injuries, and the broader context of their lives. The stringent application of immigration laws, devoid of consideration for individual circumstances, perpetuates a pattern of injustice and undermines the promises made to those who serve.

The lack of adequate legal representation further exacerbates the challenges faced by these veterans. Navigating the complex legal landscape of immigration law requires expertise and resources that many veterans, especially those struggling with post-service challenges, lack. The pro bono services available are often insufficient to meet the overwhelming demand, leaving many veterans vulnerable and without adequate legal representation. This deficit highlights the need for increased funding for legal aid organizations dedicated to serving the needs of non-citizen veterans.

Furthermore, the absence of a transparent and centralized process for addressing the specific immigration challenges faced by veterans creates significant delays and increases the risk of deportation. The current system, characterized by fragmented processes and a lack of interagency coordination, forces veterans to navigate a labyrinthine bureaucratic system, often without adequate support or guidance. This convoluted system leads to unnecessary delays, increasing the likelihood of adverse outcomes and perpetuating a cycle of uncertainty and fear.

The cases looked at above to expose the systemic failings that must be addressed as soon as possible. The rigid application of immigration laws without accounting for the realities of military service and the unique challenges faced by veterans is fundamentally unjust. The lack of sufficient legal aid and a streamlined, veteran-centric process compound these problems. From now on, a multi-pronged approach is essential. This necessitates legislative reforms to incorporate compassionate considerations for service-related issues, increased funding for legal aid for veterans, and the establishment of a dedicated agency or program within the Department of Veterans Affairs (VA) or Department of Homeland Security (DHS) responsible for coordinating the immigration concerns of non-citizen veterans. The collaborative effort must involve increased training for immigration judges and officials on the specific challenges veterans face, fostering a more nuanced and informed approach to decision-making.

International comparisons reveal that other countries have implemented more comprehensive and equitable systems for addressing the immigration needs of their veterans. Many nations afford their military personnel – citizens and non-citizens – more excellent legal protection, recognizing their contributions and acknowledging the unique vulnerabilities they may face upon returning to civilian life. Examining these successful models could provide valuable insights and inform potential reforms in the United States.

In conclusion, the case studies highlight the profound human consequences of a system that fails to honor the service and sacrifices of non-citizen veterans. The stories presented illustrate the legal challenges and the emotional toll of facing deportation after serving one's country. It is a moral imperative to reform this system, ensuring that the promises made to those who serve are upheld and that these veterans are treated with the respect, dignity, and gratitude they deserve. Only through comprehensive legislative action and a fundamental shift in perspective can we hope to repair the damage done and prevent future instances of such injustice.

The fight for fair and equitable treatment of non-citizen veterans is far from over, but the stories shared here serve as a powerful reminder of the stakes involved and the urgent need for action. The systemic failures revealed in these case studies underscore the critical need for systemic reform, not merely as a matter of legal compliance but as a testament to our moral obligations to those who have served and sacrificed for our nation.

8 / THE CHALLENGES OF PROCESSING AND APPEALS

The stark reality facing non-citizen veterans, as illustrated in the previous chapter's case studies, extends far beyond the initial legal battles. The fight for their right to remain in the United States often continues through a complex and frequently frustrating appeals process, mired in bureaucratic obstacles designed, it seems, to hinder rather than facilitate justice. This labyrinthine system, built upon layers of regulations and interpretations, actively works against the individuals who have pledged their allegiance and risked their lives for this nation.

The initial deportation order, often delivered with little prior warning or explanation, is the first hurdle. The process of appealing such an order is a daunting task, demanding an understanding of intricate legal codes and procedures far beyond the grasp of most individuals, especially those who may be grappling with the psychological trauma of combat or the emotional strain of impending deportation. The sheer volume of paperwork alone can be overwhelming, requiring the compilation of extensive documentation, including military records, immigration records, and personal testimonials, all often scattered across multiple agencies and jurisdictions. The burden of proof rests heavily on the veteran, demanding a meticulous and comprehensive presentation of their case, a task made significantly more difficult by limited resources and access to legal representation.

The lack of readily accessible legal aid significantly contributes to the difficulties non-citizen veterans face navigating the appeals process. While pro bono services exist, they are often oversubscribed, leaving many veterans representing themselves as inherently unequal, given the complexity of immigration law. This leaves them vulnerable to errors in procedure or insufficient presentation of evidence, often leading to the denial of their appeal. The financial burden associated with legal counsel adds another layer of hardship, forcing veterans to choose between hiring an attorney and providing for their families, a stark choice few should ever have to make.

Beyond the challenges of assembling evidence and securing legal representation, the sheer length and uncertainty of the appeals process itself contribute to the psychological toll on veterans. The waiting period can stretch for years, during which veterans live in a state of constant anxiety, unsure of their future, and facing the ever-present threat of deportation.

This uncertainty can exacerbate existing mental health conditions, leading to depression, anxiety, and even suicidal ideation. The lack of consistent communication from immigration authorities adds to the stress, leaving veterans in a state of information limbo, unable to plan for their future or find a sense of stability.

Furthermore, there are inconsistencies in the application of immigration laws and regulations that exacerbate the difficulties veterans face in their appeals. The decisions of immigration judges can often seem arbitrary, with similar cases resulting in vastly different outcomes. This inconsistency stems from the complex and frequently contradictory nature of immigration law, which allows for significant discretion by immigration officials. While intended to allow for nuanced consideration of individual circumstances, this discretion often leads to unpredictable and unfair results, particularly for veterans who may have served with distinction but are subjected to disparate treatment due to minor offenses or procedural errors.

The interaction between different government agencies further complicates the appeals process. The Department of Homeland Security (DHS), responsible for immigration enforcement, often operates in isolation from the Department of Veterans Affairs (VA), which supports veterans' needs.

This lack of inter-agency cooperation creates significant challenges for veterans seeking to demonstrate their service and eligibility for relief. Often, information critical to their appeal remains siloed within different agencies, hindering the efficient processing of their cases and leading to unnecessary delays. The lack of a straightforward and streamlined communication channel between these agencies results in veterans navigating a confusing and inefficient bureaucratic maze, often repeating the same information multiple times to different officials.

Another significant hurdle is the lack of clarity and consistency in interpreting and applying the laws and regulations governing the immigration status of non-citizen veterans. The legal framework is characterized by ambiguities and contradictions, leading to differing interpretations by immigration officials and judges. This lack of clarity often results in inconsistent application of the laws, leading to unpredictable outcomes in individual cases and exacerbating the stress and uncertainty veterans face.

The inherent power imbalance between the individual veteran and the government further compounds the complexities of the appeals pro. With its vast resources and legal expertise, the government holds a significantly advantageous position in these proceedings. Veterans, often lacking the resources and expertise to challenge government decisions effectively, are left at a distinct disadvantage. This imbalance further underscores the urgent need for reform to ensure fair and equitable treatment.

The potential for procedural errors during appeals adds another layer of complexity and injustice. A minor oversight or procedural mistake, often due to a lack of legal expertise, can lead to a veteran's appeal, regardless of the merits of their case. The rejection of accessible legal support and guidance increases the likelihood of such errors, compounding veterans' challenges.

Moreover, the emotional and psychological impact of navigating this complex and protracted system cannot be overstated. The prolonged uncertainty, the repeated setbacks, and the constant threat of deportation can have a devastating impact on the mental and physical well-being of veterans, exacerbating existing conditions and creating new challenges. The lack of empathy and support from the system only serves to amplify this suffering.

Examples abound of veterans who have been entangled in this bureaucratic nightmare despite years of exemplary service. Cases involving minor offenses, such as traffic violations or drug-related incidents, often lead to deportation orders despite substantial evidence of service and character.

The lack of proportionality in sentencing, the emphasis on technicalities rather than context, and the absence of comprehensive consideration of individual circumstances contribute to the unfair and unjust outcomes observed.

In conclusion, the bureaucratic obstacles encountered by non-citizen veterans in appealing deportation orders are significant and systematic. The lack of access to legal aid, the lengthy and uncertain process, the inconsistencies in legal interpretation and application, and the inherent power imbalance all contribute to a system that often seems designed to fail those who have served their country with distinction. Reforming this system requires a multi-pronged approach, addressing the legal complexities and the human cost of these bureaucratic failures. We hope to ensure fair and equitable treatment for these often-overlooked patriots only through concerted legislative action and a fundamental shift in perspective. The path to justice for non-citizen veterans is long and arduous, but the fight must continue. The stories of their struggles serve as a powerful testament to the urgent need for meaningful reform, highlighting the profound moral obligation to honor their service and uphold the promises made to them. The ongoing injustices demand immediate attention and decisive action from legislative and bureaucratic bodies.

9 / ACCESS TO JUSTICE

The systemic challenges faced by non-citizen veterans extend beyond the labyrinthine appeals process; they are deeply intertwined with the stark disparities in access to legal representation. This inequality fundamentally undermines the promise of due process and significantly impacts deportation outcomes. While the right to legal counsel is a cornerstone of the American justice system, its reality for non-citizen veterans facing deportation is often far removed from this ideal. Many lack the financial resources to secure competent legal representation, leaving them navigating the complexities of immigration law largely alone, ill-equipped to understand the nuances of their cases and the strategies necessary for a successful defense.

The financial burden of immigration proceedings is substantial. Legal fees, including initial consultations, filing fees, and representation throughout the various stages of the process – from initial hearings to appeals – can quickly reach tens of thousands of dollars. For many veterans, especially those struggling with the physical or mental health consequences of their service or those who have experienced homelessness or unemployment after leaving the military, these costs are insurmountable. The lack of sufficient savings, coupled with the often-delayed or denied veterans' benefits, places them at a severe disadvantage from the outset. This economic disparity creates a two-tiered system of justice, where those with access to expensive legal counsel have a significantly higher chance of a favorable outcome than those forced to navigate the system pro se, often with disastrous consequences.

Furthermore, the geographical distribution of legal aid organizations specializing in immigration law exacerbates this inequality. Many veterans reside in areas with limited access to pro bono services or affordable legal aid, leaving few options beyond expensive private attorneys. Rural communities, in particular, are often underserved, leaving veterans in these areas disproportionately vulnerable to deportation due to their inability to secure adequate representation. Even in areas with more robust legal aid networks, the limited resources often mean long waitlists and high demand for services, resulting in many veterans not receiving timely or adequate legal assistance. The sheer volume of cases and the complexities of immigration law make it incredibly challenging for overburdened legal aid organizations to meet the needs of all those who seek their help.

The consequences of inadequate legal representation are far-reaching and devastating. Without a skilled attorney to navigate the intricacies of immigration law, veterans often miss crucial deadlines, fail to submit necessary documentation, and cannot effectively argue their case. This can lead to incorrect legal interpretations, missed opportunities for relief, and, ultimately, deportation. The lack of understanding of procedural rules and evidentiary standards can also significantly impact the outcome of their cases, further compounding the injustice they face. A competent attorney can often identify and exploit weaknesses in the government's case, introduce mitigating evidence such as military service records, and effectively argue for alternative forms of relief, such as cancellation of removal or adjustment of status. Without this legal expertise, these opportunities are often lost, resulting in the deportation of individuals who may otherwise have been eligible to remain in the country.

The psychological toll of navigating the immigration system without adequate legal representation cannot be overstated. The fear of deportation, the uncertainty of the legal process, and the constant threat of separation from family and community can have profound and long-lasting effects on mental health. Veterans, already potentially burdened with PTSD, traumatic brain injuries, or other service-connected disabilities, face an additional layer of trauma as they struggle to secure their legal status. This further highlights the inadequacy of the current system and its failure to recognize and address the unique vulnerabilities of this population. The lack of access to appropriate mental health care exacerbates these issues, creating a vicious cycle of hardship and disadvantage.

The impact on families is also profound. Deportation separates families, fracturing communities and disrupting the lives of spouses, children, and extended family members. The economic consequences of a deported parent or spouse can be devastating, leaving families struggling to make ends meet and cope with the emotional trauma of separation. The children of deported veterans may face academic and emotional challenges, potentially suffering long-term negative consequences from the absence of a parent. The ripple effects of these deportations extend far beyond the individual veteran, underscoring the systemic failures that not only violate the rights of the veteran but also inflict considerable hardship on their loved ones.

The issue of legal representation is not simply a matter of

individual responsibility but a reflection of systemic failures within the immigration system. The lack of sufficient funding for legal aid organizations, the complexity and opacity of immigration laws, and the lack of proactive measures to ensure access to justice for vulnerable populations all contribute to this disparity. Furthermore, the inherent power imbalance between the individual and the state in immigration proceedings further disadvantages those without adequate representation. With its vast resources and legal expertise, the government is often better equipped to navigate the system's complexities, while individuals without proper legal counsel are at a significant disadvantage. The system usually defaults to an adversarial model, hindering the ability of non-citizen veterans to present their cases effectively.

International comparisons further highlight the shortcomings of the US system. Many other developed countries provide more robust legal aid systems and greater access to legal representation for immigrants facing deportation, particularly those with a history of military service. These countries often recognize the unique contributions of immigrant veterans and offer more comprehensive support systems to assist them in navigating the legal and bureaucratic challenges they face. These contrasting approaches underscore the need for significant reform in the US system to align with international best practices and ensure fair and equitable treatment for all veterans, regardless of their citizenship status.

Addressing this disparity requires a multifaceted approach. Increased funding for legal aid organizations specializing in immigration law is crucial. This funding should be specifically targeted to support those organizations providing services to veterans, ensuring they have the resources to meet the high service demand. Moreover, initiatives for pro bono legal services should be expanded and strengthened. Collaboration between veterans' organizations and legal aid providers can effectively connect veterans with much-needed legal assistance. Simplifying the immigration legal process, streamlining bureaucratic procedures, and providing clear and accessible information about legal rights and options can also significantly improve access to justice. Providing legal aid information in multiple languages, mainly those prevalent among non-citizen veteran communities, is essential to ensure inclusivity and equitable access to justice.

Furthermore, legislative reforms are necessary to address the underlying systemic inequalities. Expanding eligibility criteria for government-funded legal aid programs and creating more robust support networks for non-citizen veterans would significantly improve their access to legal representation. This may involve creating specialized legal aid programs specifically designed to meet the unique needs of non-citizen veterans or providing funding to expand existing veterans' legal assistance programs to incorporate immigration law. Additionally, policy changes that focus on streamlining bureaucratic processes and reducing delays in the deportation process could also help to lessen the burden on veterans. The goal should be to establish a more efficient and equitable system that ensures every non-citizen veteran has access to quality legal representation, regardless of their financial resources.

Ultimately, ensuring equal access to legal representation is not just a matter of fairness but a moral imperative. These individuals have distinguishedly served our nation, risking their lives to defend our freedoms. To deny them access to justice, leaving them vulnerable to deportation due to their inability to afford legal counsel, is a profound betrayal of the promises made to them and a disgrace to the values this nation claims to uphold. Addressing the disparities in legal representation requires a concerted effort from all stakeholders – government agencies, legal aid organizations, veterans' groups, and the public – to ensure that every non-citizen veteran receives the fair and equitable treatment they deserve. Only through comprehensive and sustained reform can we hope to fulfill the promises made to these often-overlooked patriots and restore integrity to our justice system.

10 / MINOR OFFENSES AND DEPORTATION

The stark reality for many non-citizen veterans is that even minor offenses, seemingly insignificant infractions in the context of a life dedicated to service, can trigger the devastating process of deportation. This is a fierce irony, given these individuals' sacrifices for the nation. The intersection of criminal justice and immigration law creates a complex and unforgiving system where a single misstep can outweigh years of loyal service and unwavering commitment regardless of severity.

The legal framework governing deportation is vast and intricate, often leaving veterans bewildered and vulnerable. While the intent behind immigration laws is ostensibly to protect national security and maintain order, the application of these laws usually disproportionately affects non-citizen veterans, who may lack the resources and understanding necessary to navigate the complexities of the system. Even minor traffic violations, such as driving under the influence or a series of minor speeding tickets, can accumulate to trigger the scrutiny of immigration authorities, leading to detention and deportation proceedings. Similarly, drug-related offenses, even those stemming from youthful indiscretions or stemming from post-traumatic stress disorder (PTSD) and self-medication, can have profoundly damaging consequences.

The lack of clarity and consistency in applying these laws exacerbates the problem. Discrepancies in how different judges and immigration officials interpret and apply regulations create a climate of uncertainty and unpredictability, leaving veterans vulnerable to inconsistent outcomes. What might result in a lenient sentence for one Individual could lead to deportation for another, despite similar offenses and backgrounds. This lack of transparency undermines the principles of justice and fairness that our legal system should uphold.

Furthermore, the burden of proof often lies heavily on the veteran to demonstrate their eligibility to remain in the country. This requires not only a deep understanding of immigration law – an area often beyond the expertise of most individuals – but also the ability to gather and present extensive documentation, often spanning many years. The sheer complexity of this task, coupled with the emotional and financial strain of facing deportation, can be overwhelming for even the most resilient individuals. This burden is especially acute for veterans who may be grappling with PTSD or other mental health challenges resulting from their service, making it difficult to navigate the complex bureaucratic processes involved.

The impact of this unequal application of the law is felt not only by the veterans themselves but also by their families and communities. The separation of families, the loss of employment, and the disruption of established social networks are significant consequences that ripple far beyond the individual. Children of deported veterans often face the trauma of parental separation, while the loss of a veteran's contributions to their communities creates a societal void.

Consider the case of a non-citizen veteran who served multiple tours in Iraq or Afghanistan, receiving commendations for bravery and dedication. Upon returning home, this veteran may struggle to readjust to civilian life, experiencing difficulties finding employment and dealing with the lingering effects of PTSD. If this veteran, in a moment of vulnerability, commits a minor offense, such as driving while intoxicated, the consequences could be devastating. Rather than receiving support and treatment for their mental health challenges, these veterans might find themselves facing deportation, separated from their families and the nation they so valiantly served.

Another example could be a veteran who, while struggling with the financial burden of transitioning back to civilian life, commits a minor drug offense. The possession of a small amount of marijuana, perhaps for self-medication to cope with PTSD, could trigger the immigration machinery, leading to a lengthy deportation process, stripping away the opportunities and stability that this veteran worked so hard to achieve.

The lack of adequate legal representation further exacerbates the situation. Many non-citizen veterans cannot afford skilled legal counsel to guide them through the intricacies of the immigration system. This inequality of access to justice exacerbates their already daunting challenges, leaving them to navigate a complex and often hostile legal environment alone. The pro bono services available are usually overwhelmed, leaving many veterans without the legal assistance they desperately need.

Another critical factor is the lack of culturally competent legal aid. Veterans from diverse backgrounds may find it even harder to access effective legal representation that understands their unique circumstances and cultural nuances.

Language barriers and the lack of legal assistance services tailored to the needs of specific communities can lead to a lack of understanding of their legal rights and increase the risk of deportation.

Beyond the individual cases, the broader societal implications of deporting non-citizen veterans are far-reaching. The nation loses the contributions of individuals who have served and sacrificed, often facing the risk of severe injury or even death, in defense of their values and interests. The loss of their skills, experience, and potential impact negatively affects the economy and society.

This issue underscores a critical failure in the system's obligation to protect and support those who have served in the military. The failure to provide adequate legal representation, coupled with the disproportionate application of immigration law, constitutes a profound betrayal of the implicit promise made to those who risk their lives in service to their country. It highlights a disconnect between the rhetoric of gratitude and the reality of experience for non-citizen veterans. Addressing this systemic failure requires a multifaceted approach, encompassing changes to immigration law, increased access to legal representation, and a broader cultural shift in how we value and support those who have served in the military, regardless of their citizenship status. Ignoring this issue is not only ethically reprehensible but also strategically unwise, as it undermines the very principles of loyalty and commitment that we expect from our soldiers. The reform needed is not merely a matter of legal technicality but a moral imperative. The United States must ensure that its commitment to its veterans extends beyond mere words and that the promises made are upheld with the same unwavering resolve that these veterans have shown in service to their adopted nation. The long-term consequences of failing to address this issue will likely overshadow any short-term gains.

11 / THE HUMAN TOLL OF DEPORTATION

The forced separation from family and community inflicted by deportation constitutes a profound and often overlooked human cost. This severance carries a particular weight for non-citizen veterans, given their prior commitment to the United States and the expectation of reciprocal support. The impact extends far beyond the individual, rippling through familial networks and disrupting established social connections. The immediate consequence is often the agonizing physical separation from spouses, children, parents, and siblings. This separation is not simply a geographical distance; it represents the shattering of deeply ingrained emotional bonds, leading to profound feelings of loss, grief, and isolation. The emotional toll on family members left behind is substantial, often resulting in financial hardship, emotional distress, and a pervasive sense of abandonment. Children, in particular, may experience significant developmental challenges, struggling with separation anxiety, trauma, and a diminished sense of security. The disruption of parental roles further exacerbates these difficulties, potentially resulting in long-term psychological and emotional scars.

The effects extend beyond the immediate family unit.

Many non-citizen veterans have cultivated extensive support networks within their local communities. These networks, comprising friends, neighbors, fellow veterans, and religious congregations, provide crucial social, emotional, and often practical support. Deportation dismantles these vital networks, leaving the individual isolated and vulnerable in a new and unfamiliar environment. The loss of this community support can significantly hinder their ability to socially and economically reintegrate. The experience of deportation often results in feelings of shame, stigma, and a profound sense of betrayal. This is particularly acute for veterans who have served their adopted country with loyalty and dedication, only to be cast aside and ostracized. The lack of understanding and empathy from their former communities, compounded by the trauma of deportation, can deepen their feelings of alienation and isolation.

The challenges extend beyond the emotional and social spheres. Deportation often precipitates a severe economic downturn for both the deported individual and their remaining family members. The loss of employment in the United States and the difficulties of finding comparable work at home can often lead to financial insecurity and hardship.

Many deported veterans struggle to find suitable housing, access healthcare, and provide for their families' basic needs.

The lack of economic stability intensifies the emotional distress and contributes to an overall decline in well-being. Moreover, the skills and experience acquired during military service may not translate easily to employment opportunities in the home country, further exacerbating the economic challenges. This lack of financial stability and access to resources can lead to a cycle of poverty and dependence, perpetuating the negative impacts of deportation across generations.

The challenges of reintegration into their home countries

are often immense. Even in cases where veterans return to their countries of origin, they may face significant hurdles in adapting to a society that has changed since their departure. The cultural adjustments, coupled with the emotional trauma of deportation and the absence of familiar support networks, can prove overwhelming. Many may struggle to reconnect with their former lives and find their place within their home communities. They may also encounter prejudice and discrimination based on their previous residency in the United States or because their experiences during military service have fundamentally altered their perspective and relationship with their country of origin. Language barriers, different cultural norms, and unfamiliarity with the local systems can further complicate the reintegration process.

Many deported veterans feel lost and adrift, struggling to establish a stable life after the disruption caused by deportation.

The disruption caused by deportation isn't merely a one-time event; its impact reverberates. The long-term consequences for deported veterans and their families are profound and far-reaching. The emotional scars of separation, coupled with the economic hardship and challenges of reintegration, can have a lasting effect on mental and physical health, educational attainment, and social mobility. The loss of social support systems and the trauma of deportation can contribute to long-term psychological distress, including increased rates of depression, anxiety, and post-traumatic stress disorder (PTSD). Furthermore, disrupting family structures and educational pathways can impact children's academic achievement, social adjustment, and overall well-being. The intergenerational impact of deportation must be critically considered, as the consequences for children and future generations may be even more significant and challenging to overcome. This long-term perspective emphasizes the necessity for policy changes to prevent these widespread and often devastating consequences.

The personal narratives of deported veterans paint a poignant picture of the devastating effects of deportation. Often filled with grief, anger, and a profound sense of injustice, these accounts highlight the human cost of flawed immigration policies. One common theme that emerges from interviews is the feeling of betrayal. Many veterans believed their service to the United States would lead to citizenship or protection from deportation. The discovery that their sacrifices were not reciprocated leads to a profound sense of disillusionment and betrayal, which can have a profound and lasting effect on their mental well-being. The process is frequently described as dehumanizing, characterized by bureaucratic indifference, delays in legal processes, and a lack of compassion. Many veterans recount experiencing feelings of isolation, helplessness, and profound hopelessness during the process. The loss of their identity as veterans, coupled with the difficulties of assimilation in their new environments, further exacerbates their feelings of powerlessness.

These accounts frequently describe the difficulties of maintaining contact with their families, including the financial burden of phone calls and visits. Many veterans are unable to provide financial support to their loved ones, adding to the emotional distress and creating further strains on relationships. Moreover, the difficulties of navigating new cultures and unfamiliar legal systems in their home countries often lead to additional feelings of isolation and vulnerability. The stories also frequently highlight the loss of purpose and meaning after leaving the United States and the absence of the sense of belonging and camaraderie they experienced while in service. These narratives underscore the importance of considering not just the legal and procedural aspects of deportation but also the profound human cost of these actions. They demonstrate the urgency of addressing the systemic issues that lead to the deportation of non-citizen veterans and the importance of creating policies that are both just and compassionate.

The systematic failures that contribute to the deportation of non-citizen veterans are interwoven and complex. They encompass the shortcomings of immigration laws, bureaucratic inefficiencies, and the lack of adequate legal representation. Moreover, the often-overlooked role of criminal justice in the deportation process highlights how seemingly minor offenses can trigger deportation proceedings, regardless of a veteran's military service. The absence of robust support networks and resources for deported veterans only exacerbates the challenges they face. Addressing these systemic failures requires a multi-pronged approach encompassing legislative reform, improved bureaucratic processes, and increased access to legal assistance. It also requires a shift in public understanding and perception of non-citizen veterans, recognizing their contributions and addressing the nation's ethical obligation towards those who have served in its armed forces.

The scale of the problem demands a comprehensive and multi-faceted approach. Policy reforms must prioritize the well-being of non-citizen veterans, ensuring they receive fair and equitable treatment. Legislative changes should address the inconsistencies in immigration laws, preventing minor offenses from leading to deportation. Improvements in bureaucratic procedures are also crucial, ensuring that cases are processed efficiently and transparently and offering veterans timely access to legal support and representation.

Increased access to legal aid is essential for providing non-citizen veterans with the resources they need to navigate the complex immigration system.

Furthermore, creating support networks and resources for

deported veterans is crucial. These will aid their reintegration into their home countries and assist them with the economic and social challenges they face. Addressing this issue requires a commitment to upholding the nation's promise to its veterans, regardless of their citizenship status.

The United States can only fulfill its ethical obligations to these often-overlooked patriots and their families through systemic change and public awareness.

12 / PTSD AND THE STRESS OF DEPORTATION

The profound disruption caused by deportation extends far beyond the immediate physical separation from loved ones; it profoundly impacts the mental well-being of non-citizen veterans, often triggering or exacerbating pre-existing mental health conditions. Many of these veterans have already endured significant trauma during their military service, potentially leading to Post-Traumatic Stress Disorder (PTSD) and other trauma-related disorders. The added stress of deportation is an important trigger, intensifying these conditions and creating a cascade of negative consequences.

The loss of familiar support systems, the uncertainty of the future, and the overwhelming sense of betrayal by the nation they served can push individuals to the brink, leading to increased rates of depression, anxiety, and substance abuse.

The process of deportation itself is frequently traumatic, involving detention, separation from family, and often the harrowing experience of being forcibly removed from a country they consider home. This can further traumatize individuals who have already experienced significant adversity, compounding existing mental health vulnerabilities.

The absence of consistent and accessible mental health support further complicates the situation. Many deported veterans lack access to adequate healthcare in their home countries, leaving them struggling to cope with their mental health challenges without professional assistance. Even if services exist, language barriers, cultural differences, and the financial burden of accessing these services can create insurmountable obstacles. The lack of continuity of care between the United States and the receiving country also severely hampers effective treatment. Veterans who were receiving treatment in the US often find themselves without support upon deportation, forcing them to navigate an entirely new healthcare system, often with limited resources and understanding of their specific needs.

The social stigma associated with mental illness further exacerbates the situation. In some cultures, mental health conditions are viewed with considerable stigma and shame, leading to reluctance to seek help or disclose mental health struggles. This reluctance can result in untreated mental health issues that worsen over time, impacting their overall well-being and ability to reintegrate into their home communities. Deportation further isolates these individuals, severing their connection to support networks and increasing feelings of shame and hopelessness. The loss of social connections combined with existing mental health challenges can create a perfect storm, significantly increasing the risk of self-harm and suicide.

Consider, for instance, the case of a veteran who served multiple tours in Afghanistan, witnessing intense combat and experiencing significant loss within his unit. He returns to the United States, struggles with PTSD, and receives treatment through the Veterans Administration. However, due to a minor offense unrelated to his military service—perhaps driving under the influence charge—he faces deportation. The trauma of deportation, coupled with the sudden cessation of his treatment, triggers a severe relapse. He is deported to a country he barely remembers, where he faces immense challenges in accessing adequate mental health care. The linguistic and cultural barriers further isolate him, deepening his feelings of alienation and despair. His story is not an anomaly but a tragic example of the systemic failures that leave vulnerable veterans without the support they desperately need.

The impact of PTSD on deported veterans is particularly severe given the complexities of reintegrating into a new environment, often with limited resources and understanding. The symptoms of PTSD—nightmares, flashbacks, hypervigilance, and avoidance—can be intensely debilitating, making it difficult to hold a job, maintain relationships, or even navigate daily life. For veterans who find themselves in unfamiliar cultural contexts, these symptoms can be amplified, triggering feelings of intense anxiety and disorientation. The lack of familiarity with the language, customs, and social norms can lead to further isolation and feelings of helplessness.

The challenges extend beyond PTSD. Deported veterans often suffer from depression, anxiety, and substance use disorders. These conditions are frequently interconnected, with each exacerbating the others. Depression can lead to isolation and hopelessness, increasing the risk of substance abuse as a coping mechanism. Similarly, anxiety can worsen PTSD symptoms, making it even more challenging to function and interact with the world. The cumulative effect of these conditions can be devastating, leading to long-term disability and a severely diminished quality of life.

Moreover, the economic difficulties faced by deported veterans often worsen their mental health. Many struggle to find employment in their home countries, facing unemployment and financial instability. This economic hardship can significantly affect their access to healthcare, housing, and other essential resources. The stress of financial instability, coupled with the emotional burden of deportation and pre-existing mental health challenges, can create a vicious cycle of poverty and distress, making it even more challenging to recover. The absence of social safety nets in many countries exacerbates the precariousness of their situation.

International comparisons highlight the need for a more humane and comprehensive approach to supporting non-citizen veterans. Some countries have implemented robust programs to provide comprehensive mental health services to veterans, regardless of their citizenship status. These programs often include culturally sensitive mental health services, language support, and financial assistance to ensure equitable access to care. The United States could learn valuable lessons from these international models, such as adapting and integrating best practices to improve its support system for deported veterans.

The failure to provide adequate mental health support to deported veterans constitutes a moral and ethical failing.

These individuals served their country with courage and dedication, making sacrifices that most citizens cannot comprehend. They deserve to be treated with dignity and respect, and that includes access to comprehensive mental health care. The systemic negligence that leaves these veterans vulnerable to the devastating consequences of PTSD and other mental health disorders demands immediate action. This necessitates a multifaceted approach involving legislative changes to ensure better access to mental health services before, during, and after deportation, increased funding for mental health initiatives specifically targeting deported veterans, and the implementation of robust programs to facilitate their reintegration into their home communities, providing cultural and linguistic support tailored to their needs. Only through such comprehensive interventions can the United States begin to address the profound human cost of its deportation policies. The current situation represents a profound betrayal of the nation's commitment to its veterans. This betrayal extends far beyond the immediate injustice of deportation to encompass the enduring and devastating consequences on their mental and Emotional well-being. The urgent need for change cannot be overstated.

13 / LOSS OF EMPLOYMENT AND SUPPORT SYSTEMS

The psychological and emotional toll of deportation, as discussed previously, is immense. However, the impact extends far beyond the realm of mental health; it plunges deported veterans and their families into a vortex of economic hardship, often with devastating and long-lasting consequences. The abrupt severance from employment, the loss of social safety nets, and the challenges of navigating a new and frequently hostile environment create a perfect storm of financial instability, leaving many struggling to meet even basic needs.

For many non-citizen veterans, their employment history in the United States is intrinsically linked to their military service. Skills acquired during their time in the armed forces, often highly specialized and valuable in civilian life, become virtually worthless upon deportation. The process of obtaining employment certifications and licenses, already complex for many, becomes insurmountable when dealing with the added hurdles of immigration status and a lack of familiarity with their new country's labor laws and regulations. These veterans, many of whom served in combat roles, find themselves ill-equipped to navigate the often unforgiving realities of the civilian job market, particularly in a new and unfamiliar environment.

Transitioning from a structured military life to the uncertainty of civilian employment is challenging for any veteran. Still, it is exponentially more challenging when faced with the added burden of deportation.

The loss of employment often translates into a complete loss of income, immediately impacting the ability to pay for housing, food, healthcare, and other essential needs. For those who were homeowners, deportation often leads to the loss of their property due to the inability to make mortgage payments. The complexities of international financial transactions, currency exchange rates, and the lack of access to banking services in their new country further complicate their economic struggles. This is particularly acute for those who may have dependents relying on their income, plunging entire families into poverty and increasing vulnerability to exploitation and other forms of harm.

The disruption of established support systems exacerbates the economic crisis. Many non-citizen veterans rely on informal support networks, including family, friends, and community organizations within their local community in the United States. Deportation abruptly severs these vital connections, leaving them isolated and without access to the crucial assistance they had previously relied upon. The emotional and practical support these networks offer—everything from childcare assistance to emotional guidance—is often irreplaceable. This isolation, coupled with economic hardship, can lead to increased vulnerability to homelessness, food insecurity, and a range of other social problems.

Furthermore, access to government assistance programs designed to help those in need becomes considerably more limited after deportation. Many veterans, even those who served honorably, lack the resources to navigate the complex bureaucratic processes of applying for assistance in their new country. Language barriers, cultural differences, and a lack of familiarity with local regulations present substantial obstacles to obtaining the help they desperately need. The transition is jarring and leaves many feeling abandoned and alone, exacerbating the financial strain. The lack of consistent support systems, particularly in the early stages of resettlement, leaves many struggling to establish themselves and often resorting to exploitative employment practices to survive.

The economic consequences also extend to the families left behind in the United States. The loss of a primary breadwinner often creates a ripple effect, impacting the family's financial stability and ability to meet basic needs.

Spouses and children are usually left to grapple with the emotional and economic burden of supporting themselves without the income and support of the deported veteran. The emotional toll on family members is significant, and the financial struggles can lead to a cascade of negative consequences, such as increased rates of poverty, food insecurity, and even homelessness.

In addition to the immediate loss of income, the long-term economic consequences of deportation are equally devastating. The lack of access to education, employment opportunities, and healthcare in their new country can create a cycle of poverty that extends for generations. The ability to accumulate savings or build wealth is often severely hampered, perpetuating economic hardship. The difficulty in obtaining credit, access to financial services, and transferring assets across borders compound their economic problems.

The financial uncertainty of their new reality leaves them

vulnerable to exploitation, pushing many into unstable or unsafe work conditions simply for survival. This instability casts a long shadow over the entire family's lives, impacting their overall well-being and ability to build a stable and secure future.

The economic hardship faced by deported veterans and their families highlights a critical flaw in the current immigration system. The lack of comprehensive support programs for deported veterans and their families, coupled with the significant challenges of navigating foreign systems and obtaining essential resources, underline a systemic failure.

It is not simply a matter of individual hardship but a reflection of a more significant societal inability to recognize and address the profound economic consequences of deportation. The issue requires a holistic approach, encompassing legislative reforms, increased funding for support programs, and improved coordination between governmental agencies to mitigate the devastating economic impacts on veterans and their families.

This economic devastation is not merely an unfortunate byproduct of deportation; it is a direct consequence of policies that fail to consider the human cost of their actions adequately. The value of the contributions of these non-citizen veterans to their communities, their families, and even to the nation itself is significantly underestimated in the context of these policies. Their contributions to the military and society are disregarded. The failure to consider the economic fallouts is a blatant disregard for the long-term consequences of these policy decisions. The long-term cost of this human suffering – healthcare expenditures, social welfare burdens, and lost productivity – is a significant financial burden on the United States and the receiving countries. A more humane and economically responsible approach would involve investing in programs that assist veterans during and after deportation, helping to ensure their financial stability and successful integration into their new communities.

The lack of consistent governmental data further complicates efforts to understand the full extent of the economic impact of deportation on veterans. Accurate data collection and analysis are crucial for informing policy decisions and developing effective interventions. The absence of such data exacerbates the problem, as it hinders the development of targeted and practical solutions. Comprehensive research is needed to fully assess the economic consequences of deportation, including the long-term impacts on individuals, families, and communities. This research must also explore effective solutions such as job training programs tailored to the skills of deported veterans, financial assistance programs, and initiatives to assist in navigating the complexities of resettlement in a new country.

Addressing the economic hardship experienced by deported veterans and their families requires a multi-faceted approach involving legislative reforms, increased funding for support services, and collaboration between government agencies and non-profit organizations. The focus must be on mitigating the financial strain, providing job training and placement assistance, supporting family members left behind, and fostering the successful reintegration of deported veterans into their new communities. This should include the creation of accessible, culturally appropriate, and multilingual support programs that are tailored to the specific needs of this vulnerable population. The failure to address these issues adequately will continue to perpetuate a cycle of poverty and hardship, underscoring the profound human and economic costs associated with the deportation of non-citizen veterans. Financial hardship is not an incidental outcome but a direct and predictable consequence of current policies. Therefore, the solution lies not in simply addressing the symptoms but in fundamentally reforming the policies that are creating the problem in the first place.

14 / INTEGRATION CHALLENGES IN HOME COUNTRIES

The social isolation and marginalization often compound the economic devastation wrought by deportation these veterans face upon their return to their home countries. For many, the idealized notion of a triumphant homecoming quickly dissolves into a harsh reality. Years spent in the U.S. military, often immersed in a distinct cultural environment, can create a significant disconnect from their home societies. This disconnect extends beyond simple cultural differences, encompassing language barriers, altered social networks, and profound alienation from a country they may barely remember.

The passage of time itself contributes to this alienation. Years spent in the United States, even decades in some cases, often lead to a weakening of familial ties and a fading familiarity with cultural norms and social expectations.

While some may maintain close relationships with family members through regular contact, the reality for many is a gradual erosion of these connections, a product of distance, differing life experiences, and the inevitable changes within families over time. Upon return, they may find themselves strangers in a familiar land, struggling to reconnect with relatives who have moved on with their lives, forging new relationships, and establishing their routines. This can be particularly acute for veterans who served during extended deployments, leaving behind families and communities that have significantly evolved during their absence.

The social landscape of their home countries may have shifted considerably since their departure. Political upheavals, economic transformations, or even simple generational shifts can create a sense of displacement and estrangement. Familiar social structures may have weakened or disappeared entirely, leaving the deported veterans struggling to find their place within a society that has fundamentally changed. This sense of not belonging can be profoundly isolating, exacerbating the psychological trauma already inflicted by the deportation process. The perceived loss of status—a veteran returning home without the accolades or recognition they might have expected—can further contribute to feelings of marginalization. The societal perception of veterans, particularly those returning from foreign wars, can vary significantly across cultures. In some societies, veterans might be revered and celebrated, while in others, they might face stigma or distrust. This disparity in social perception further complicates the reintegration process.

Furthermore, the stigma associated with deportation itself can create significant social barriers. The act of deportation is often perceived negatively in many societies, carrying a connotation of failure, criminality, or undesirability. This can lead to social ostracization and difficulty establishing new social networks or securing employment. The deported veteran's past experiences in the US military may not translate easily into opportunities or acceptance in their home country. Their skills and training, while potentially valuable, might not be recognized or applicable within the local job market. This lack of economic opportunity can further perpetuate social isolation, trapping them in a cycle of marginalization and poverty.

Language barriers can act as a significant impediment to successful reintegration. Years of living and working in an English-speaking environment can lead to declining fluency in their native language. This linguistic challenge can affect their ability to communicate effectively with family members, find employment, access essential services, and navigate everyday life. This difficulty in communication can lead to frustration, isolation, and feelings of helplessness, compounding the existing psychological and social pressures.

The absence of support networks also exacerbates the challenges faced by deported veterans. The U.S. military provides a structured support system for its personnel, including access to healthcare, counseling, and social services. The sudden absence of this support upon deportation leaves many veterans vulnerable and alone. The lack of access to similar services in their home country can significantly hinder their ability to cope with the challenges of reintegration, leaving them grappling with emotional trauma, economic hardship, and social isolation without the necessary resources for assistance.

The nature of the deportation – often abrupt and without adequate preparation – contributes significantly to these challenges. Many deported veterans have little or no time to plan their return, secure housing, or arrange for employment.

This lack of preparation leaves them vulnerable and ill-equipped to navigate the complexities of reintegrating into a new and potentially hostile environment. The emotional shock of deportation, coupled with the immediate practical challenges of finding shelter and securing necessities, can further overwhelm individuals already grappling with the psychological trauma of their ordeal.

The absence of government assistance or the inadequacy of

existing programs worsens the situation. Many governments do not have well-established support systems specifically designed to assist deported veterans. This absence of targeted support highlights a significant gap in post-deportation care, leaving these individuals to navigate complex challenges mainly independently. Even when support programs do exist, language barriers, bureaucratic hurdles, and a lack of cultural sensitivity can make it difficult for deported veterans to access these resources. This inadequacy in governmental support underscores the need for policy reforms that prioritize the well-being of deported veterans and ensure their successful reintegration into their home societies.

Furthermore, the lack of adequate mental health services in their home countries presents a significant barrier. Many deported veterans have post-traumatic stress disorder (PTSD), depression, anxiety, and other mental health conditions. The absence of accessible and culturally appropriate mental healthcare services in their home countries can hinder their ability to heal and cope with the emotional toll of deportation. The stigma associated with mental illness in many societies can further discourage veterans from seeking help, leading to a cycle of untreated trauma and worsening mental health outcomes.

The complexities of reintegration extend beyond individual challenges and impact families and communities. The disruption caused by deportation extends to spouses, children, and extended family members left behind. The emotional and financial burdens faced by those left behind are significant, creating a ripple effect of hardship that extends far beyond the deported veteran. The strain on family relationships, particularly when communication becomes difficult or impossible, can create further stress and instability.

International collaboration and shared responsibility are

crucial in addressing this issue. Countries with a history of receiving deported individuals should work with sending countries to create robust support programs and ensure the successful reintegration of deported veterans. This could include joint initiatives for job training, language instruction, mental health services, and other essential support systems. A shared commitment to addressing the challenges faced by deported veterans can help mitigate the human cost of deportation and foster greater understanding and cooperation between nations.

The challenges faced by deported veterans upon their return home underscore the urgent need for a systemic shift in how deportation is handled. A more humane and comprehensive approach, recognizing the sacrifices made by these individuals and the potential for successful reintegration, is paramount. This requires not only policy reforms within the sending and receiving countries but also a fundamental reevaluation of the ethical implications of deportation policies and the responsibility of nations to support those who have served their interests abroad. The focus should shift from merely enforcing deportation to supporting the successful reintegration of deported veterans, thereby mitigating the profound social, psychological, and economic costs associated with this practice. This requires a multi-pronged strategy involving government intervention, international collaboration, and engagement from civil society organizations. Only then can we hope to reverse the devastating effects of deportation and offer these veterans the opportunity for a dignified and productive life upon their return home.

15 / VOICES OF DEPORTED VETERANS

The echoing silence of a foreign land often replaces the camaraderie of the battlefield for deported veterans. Their stories, etched with the scars of war and the sting of betrayal, paint a stark picture of the human cost of a system that seemingly forgets its promises. One veteran, a former sergeant in the U.S. Army who served two tours in Iraq, described his return to his native Mexico as a descent into a desolate landscape of disappointment. Years spent defending American ideals were abruptly replaced with the harsh reality of navigating a bureaucratic maze in a country he barely recognized, a country where his military experience held little value and his English fluency was a barrier rather than an asset. He spoke of the bewilderment of explaining his service to skeptical officials, the difficulty securing employment, and the gnawing sense of abandonment by the nation he had sworn to protect.

His experience, while unique in its details, reflects a recurring theme among deported veterans: a profound sense of alienation and loss. The transition from the structured environment of the military to the uncertainties of life in a foreign land is jarring, intensified by the emotional weight of being cast aside by the country they served. Many describe struggling with anger, betrayal, and disillusionment, compounded by the logistical challenges of re-establishing their lives. The loss of their American identity, hard-earned through years of service, is a profound and often irreparable wound. This loss extends beyond mere documentation; it encompasses the loss of a support network, the erosion of self-worth, and the crushing weight of unfulfilled expectations. They find themselves adrift in a sea of unfamiliarity, their skills and experiences often deemed Irrelevant, their hopes for a better future dashed against the rocks of indifference.

Another veteran, a former medic who served in Afghanistan, shared a poignant account of his struggle to reconcile his experiences in the military with his new reality in his home country of El Salvador. He described the emotional toll of witnessing horrific events during his deployment, only to return to a society grappling with its issues of violence and instability. Language barriers and a lack of resources hindered his attempts to access mental health services. His military experience, intended to provide a sense of purpose, had ironically contributed to his alienation. The shared experiences and camaraderie of his fellow soldiers were replaced with an isolating sense of loneliness and the constant, nagging feeling that his service had been in vain. He spoke of the difficulty in reintegrating into a society that didn't understand his experience, of the frustration of feeling that his skills and experiences were rendered useless in his new environment.

The stories of these veterans highlight the often-overlooked consequences of deportation: the psychological scars that run deeper than physical wounds. The traumatic experiences of war, coupled with the trauma of betrayal by the country they served, can lead to a cascade of mental health issues, including

PTSD, depression, and anxiety. Access to mental health services is often limited, further exacerbating their suffering. Many veterans find themselves grappling with a profound sense of loss, not only of their home in the United States but also of their identity and purpose. The support systems they relied on during their military service are often unavailable, leaving them isolated and vulnerable.

The economic hardship faced by deported veterans often amplifies their psychological distress. The lack of transferable skills, language barriers, and the absence of established support networks make finding employment incredibly challenging. This economic instability further destabilizes their lives, creating hopelessness and desperation. The transition back to their home countries is often far from the homecoming they envisioned, becoming a constant struggle for survival. For many, the idealized notion of a triumphant return home is replaced with the harsh reality of poverty and social exclusion. They find themselves struggling to provide for themselves and their families, compounding their emotional distress.

One particularly heartbreaking account came from a former Green Beret, deported to the Dominican Republic after a minor traffic offense. His story underscores the capricious nature of the immigration system and the devastating impact it has on individuals who have risked their lives for the United States. He described the surreal experience of transitioning from a highly skilled, highly trained soldier to a struggling immigrant, navigating a system he knew nothing about. The language barrier made it almost impossible to access resources or legal assistance. The support network he had built in the US military was nonexistent, rendering him entirely isolated. His economic struggles were further compounded by the absence of formal recognition for his military service, making it extremely difficult to find employment that matched his skills and experience.

Many veterans express a profound sense of being forgotten and discarded by the nation they defended. Their stories are not merely individual tales of hardship but collectively represent a systemic failure to recognize and honor the sacrifices of non-citizen veterans. The deportation of these individuals constitutes not only a betrayal of individual trust but a disregard for the nation's moral obligation to those who have risked their lives in its defense. The emotional toll of such betrayal is immense, often resulting in long-term psychological damage and social exclusion.

Furthermore, the social isolation experienced by deported veterans adds another layer to their suffering. The difficulties in communication, cultural adjustment, and the lack of understanding from their communities compound the feelings of alienation. Their military experiences, far from being assets, often become obstacles in their efforts to reintegrate into their home societies. The very skills and experiences that made them valuable soldiers usually fail to translate into the civilian world in their home countries. This sense of being an outsider, an alien in a familiar land, further intensifies their feelings of loss and abandonment.

The accounts of these deported veterans serve as a powerful reminder of the human cost of a system that prioritizes deportation over rehabilitation and recognition of service.

Their narratives underscore the urgent need for policy reforms that prioritize the well-being of these individuals and acknowledge their profound contributions to the nation.

These stories are not simply anecdotes but compelling evidence of a systemic injustice that demands immediate attention and comprehensive solutions. They call for a more humane, compassionate, and ethical approach to the issue of non-citizen veterans and the need for a national commitment to fulfilling the promises made to those who served. Their voices, often silenced, must be heard, their stories shared, and their sacrifices acknowledged to prevent further injustices.

16 / ANALYSIS AND LIMITATIONS

The Second Chance for Service Act signed into law in 2009, represented a significant, albeit imperfect, attempt to address the plight of non-citizen veterans facing deportation. The Act aimed to streamline the lawful permanent residency (green card) process for non-citizen veterans who had served honorably in the U.S. military. Before its enactment, these veterans, despite their service and sacrifice, often found themselves navigating a complex and frequently hostile immigration system, vulnerable to deportation for even minor offenses. The "Second Chance for Service Act sought to rectify this injustice by providing a more straightforward pathway to citizenship. The Act primarily focused on expediting the adjustment of status for veterans who met specific criteria, including honorable service and a period of continuous physical presence in the U.S.

However, the Act's effectiveness has been a subject of ongoing debate. While it undoubtedly facilitated the adjustment of status for some veterans, several key factors have limited its impact. Firstly, the Act's provisions are not automatic. Veterans still need to navigate the complexities of the immigration system, which can be daunting and expensive.

Many veterans lack access to legal counsel, further compounding the challenges. The cost of legal representation and the often lengthy and complicated application processes create an inherent barrier to successful application. Many deserving veterans are unable to afford the necessary legal assistance. The bureaucratic hurdles remain a significant obstacle even under the auspices of this supposedly streamlined process. Delayed processing times and inconsistent application of the law across different Immigration offices continue to create significant delays and uncertainty for applicants. Furthermore, the Act's scope is narrow. It primarily focuses on veterans who meet stringent criteria, excluding those who may have received less-than-honorable discharges or those with certain criminal convictions, even if those convictions are minor or unrelated to their military service. The definition of "honorable service" itself can be subject to interpretation, leading to further complications and potentially excluding deserving individuals. While seemingly designed to maintain standards, this restrictive definition inadvertently creates a significant hurdle for veterans who might have otherwise qualified under more flexible criteria.

The Act also fails to address the root causes of deportation among non-citizen veterans. Many veterans face deportation not due to a lack of honorable service but due to issues like minor criminal offenses, traffic violations, or immigration violations that occurred before or after their military service.

Though seemingly minor, these offenses can trigger deportation proceedings under existing immigration laws, overriding their military service and contributions to the nation. The Second Chance for Service Act does not directly address the underlying issue of how seemingly minor offenses disproportionately impact non-citizen veterans, nor does it adequately address the issue of retroactive application for past crimes.

The limitations of the Second Chance for Service Act highlight a broader systemic failure to recognize and appreciate the sacrifices of non-citizen veterans fully. The Act represents a significant step forward but is far from a complete solution. Its success hinges on factors beyond the legislation, including access to legal resources, consistent application of the law, and an overall shift in the perception of non-citizen veterans within the immigration system. The success rate of applications under the Act, while not publicly readily available in a comprehensive manner, is likely lower than ideal, pointing to the need for further improvements and a more holistic approach. The limited data available often lacks granularity, making it difficult to accurately assess the Act's effectiveness in addressing the core issues.

One critical area of concern is the lack of comprehensive data collection regarding the number of non-citizen veterans affected by deportation. The absence of this data makes it challenging to evaluate the true extent of the problem and to measure the impact of the Act and other legislative efforts.

Improved data collection and analysis are essential to formulating more effective policies. This lack of data also hinders practical advocacy efforts, as it's challenging to demonstrate the need for change without concrete numbers to support the claims. The limited and fragmented data sets often fail to capture the nuance of the individual experiences, thereby missing crucial insights into the systemic failures and personal struggles these individuals face.

Beyond the data challenges, another significant limitation stems from the adversarial nature of the immigration system itself. Even with the Act in place, many veterans find themselves facing deportation proceedings, often due to bureaucratic errors or inconsistencies in the application of the law. This points to the need for structural reform within the immigration system, shifting it away from an adversarial approach toward a more collaborative and supportive model that prioritizes the needs of veterans who have served their country. This might involve improved training for immigration officers, more precise guidelines for adjudicating cases involving veterans, and enhanced coordination between military and immigration agencies. It might also involve dedicated legal aid programs for non-citizen veterans, ensuring equitable access to justice. Moreover, the Act fails to address the long-term consequences of deportation for veterans and their families.

Deportation can lead to severe economic hardship, social isolation, and mental health challenges. These consequences are often overlooked in discussions surrounding the Act's effectiveness. Addressing these long-term consequences requires a multifaceted approach beyond providing a pathway to lawful permanent residency. It needs to include provisions for post-deportation support, such as access to mental health services, job training, and financial assistance. This more holistic approach would align with the broader ethical obligation to support veterans who have served, regardless of their immigration status.

In conclusion, while the Second Chance for Service Act represented a notable attempt to rectify the injustices faced by non-citizen veterans, its impact has been significantly limited by systemic flaws, bureaucratic hurdles, and a narrow scope. To truly address the issue, a more holistic approach is required, one that acknowledges the systemic failures within the immigration system, ensures equitable access to legal resources, addresses the root causes of deportation, and considers the long-term consequences of deportation for veterans and their families. Legislative efforts should focus on streamlining the application process and fundamentally reforming the immigration system to reflect the nation's commitment to honoring the service and sacrifice of all veterans, regardless of their citizenship status.

Further research into the challenges faced by non-citizen veterans, combined with improved data collection and analysis, is crucial to inform future legislative efforts and ensure that the promise of service and citizenship is finally fulfilled for all who have served.

17 / A REVIEW OF FEDERAL AND STATE LAWS

Beyond the Second Chance for Service Act, a patchwork of federal and state laws, regulations, and executive actions tangentially impact the immigration status of non-citizen veterans. Understanding this complex web is crucial to appreciating the full scope of these veterans' challenges. At the federal level, several statutes, while not explicitly designed for veteran immigration, nonetheless intersect with their experiences. For example, the Immigration and Nationality Act (INA) contains provisions that can be leveraged, albeit often with difficulty, to defend veterans facing deportation. Sections about waivers for certain criminal offenses, or those allowing for discretionary relief, can become focal points in legal battles to prevent deportation. However, the INA's complexity and the broad discretion afforded to immigration officials often lead to inconsistent application and unpredictable outcomes.

Furthermore, the availability of these provisions usually depends on the specific circumstances of each case, the individual's criminal history (even minor offenses can have devastating consequences), and the resources available to navigate the intricate legal process. The scarcity of pro bono legal services specifically for non-citizen veterans exacerbates this inequity.

The role of executive actions, particularly those related to Deferred Action for Childhood Arrivals (DACA) and other deferred action, should also be considered. While not directly applicable to all non-citizen veterans, such programs offer potential avenues for relief in certain situations. For instance, a veteran who arrived in the U.S. as a child and meets the DACA criteria might find a reprieve from deportation, allowing them to maintain their employment and family ties. However, the precarious nature of these programs, subject to frequent political shifts and legal challenges, renders them unreliable long-term solutions. The uncertainty inherent in relying on executive actions underscores the need for more permanent legislative protections.

At the state level, many states have enacted legislation to support veterans, some of which indirectly address immigration concerns. Several states have established veteran assistance programs that provide legal aid or other services to veterans, including those navigating the immigration system. Often funded through state budgets or grants, these programs offer crucial support. Still, their reach and effectiveness vary considerably based on funding levels, staff capacity, and the specific needs of the veteran population within each state. Moreover, the legal landscape governing veterans' benefits and services remains fragmented, with significant variations in eligibility criteria and access to resources across states. This inconsistency further highlights the need for a unified, comprehensive federal approach.

A critical aspect of this legislative landscape is the interplay between military service and criminal justice involvement. Many non-citizen veterans face deportation not because of their military service record but due to subsequent minor offenses. The seemingly incongruous juxtaposition of honorable military service with later involvement in the criminal justice system underscores the systemic flaws in both immigration and criminal justice policies. The severity of the sentencing and the implications for immigration status are often disproportionate to the actual crime committed, particularly when considering the veteran's past service and potential for rehabilitation. This necessitates a deeper examination of the potential for sentencing reform and integrating military service records into criminal sentencing considerations.

Furthermore, the lack of comprehensive data on the number of non-citizen veterans facing deportation and the specific challenges they encounter hinders effective policymaking. The existing data collection mechanisms are often fragmented and insufficient, resulting in a limited understanding of the scope and nature of the problem. Improved data collection efforts, coupled with rigorous research on the experiences of non-citizen veterans, are crucial for informing future legislative and policy initiatives.

This requires collaboration among various agencies, including the Department of Defense, the Department of Homeland Security, and the Department of Veterans Affairs, to create a more unified and comprehensive data system. The lack of adequate legal representation significantly impacts the outcomes for non-citizen veterans facing deportation. Many struggle to afford legal counsel, leaving them vulnerable to deportation without proper defense. The pro bono legal services available cannot often meet the high demand, creating a significant access-to-justice gap.

Addressing this requires increased investment in pro bono legal services designed to assist non-citizen veterans and initiatives to learn about their rights and to educate vete available legal resources. Furthermore, streamlined legal processes and more precise guidelines could make it easier for veterans to navigate the complexities of the immigration system, even without legal representation.

Another crucial aspect lies in the international comparison of policies towards non-citizen veterans. Many countries offer more streamlined pathways to citizenship for those who have served in their armed forces, highlighting the potential for policy improvements in the U.S. Examining best practices in other nations, particularly those with similar immigration challenges, can provide valuable insights and potential solutions. This comparative analysis should consider various factors, such as the specific criteria for citizenship, the procedures involved, and the overall effectiveness of these policies in integrating non-citizen veterans into society. Learning from the successes and failures of other countries could inform future legislative changes and lead to more effective policies in the U.S.

The analysis of state-level legislative attempts reveals a varied landscape of support for veterans, ranging from direct financial assistance to legal aid services. Some states have established dedicated veterans' affairs offices with expertise in immigration matters, providing crucial support to non-citizen veterans navigating the complex legal landscape.

However, the lack of uniformity across states creates inconsistencies in the level and type of assistance offered, resulting in inequitable access to resources. A standardized approach, facilitated by federal legislation and funding, is essential to ensure equitable treatment of non-citizen veterans across all states. The issue of non-citizen veterans facing deportation is not simply a matter of immigration policy; it's a question of national commitment and ethical responsibility. These individuals have sworn an oath to defend the nation, often facing significant personal risks. Their subsequent vulnerability to deportation casts a shadow on the nation's promises and undermines the very principles upon which military service is based. Therefore, a comprehensive solution requires reviewing and improving existing legislation and a fundamental shift in the national perspective on the value and commitment to those who have served, regardless of their citizenship status. The ongoing debates surrounding these issues underscore the need for a continued critical examination of current policies and a commitment to crafting a system that truly honors the sacrifices of all who serve. The path forward necessitates a holistic approach that includes legislative reform, increased funding for legal aid, improved data collection, and a broader societal acknowledgment of the debt owed to these often-overlooked patriots.

18 / IMPROVING THE SYSTEM FOR NON-CITIZEN VETERANS

The current system demonstrably fails non-citizen veterans, leaving them vulnerable to deportation despite their service. Addressing this requires a multi-pronged approach encompassing legislative reform, increased funding for legal assistance, enhanced data collection and analysis, and a fundamental shift in societal perception. The recommendations outlined below aim to create a more just and equitable system that honors the sacrifices of all who serve, regardless of their immigration status.

First, we must streamline and clarify the pathways to citizenship for non-citizen veterans. The current process is convoluted and often inaccessible, leaving many veterans trapped in a bureaucratic labyrinth. A dedicated, expedited naturalization process specifically for veterans, with simplified application procedures and reduced processing times, is crucial. This should include a clear, easily understood checklist of requirements and readily available resources to assist veterans in navigating the application process. Moreover, the process should be proactively advertised within the military and veteran support organizations to ensure veterans know their eligibility and available support. This proactive outreach is essential, given that many non-citizen veterans may not fully understand their rights or the complexities of the immigration system.

Second, legislative reforms are needed to address the disproportionate impact of minor criminal offenses on non-citizen veterans' immigration status. The current system often equates minor infractions with significant immigration consequences, leading to deportation despite years of honorable service. Specific legislative amendments should be introduced to establish a more precise standard for evaluating the severity of offenses in the context of veteran status and military service. This could involve creating a tiered system, differentiating between offenses that directly relate to national security or pose a significant threat to public safety and those that are minor, non-violent, and do not reflect a pattern of criminal behavior. The amendments should also provide a precise mechanism for veterans to demonstrate rehabilitation and their commitment to law-abiding citizenship. Furthermore, the process should prioritize individualized evaluations, considering factors such as the veteran's military record, length of service, and contributions to society. The focus should be on rehabilitation and reintegration rather than punitive measures.

Third, significant investment in legal aid for non-citizen veterans is indispensable. Many veterans lack the financial resources to access competent legal representation, leaving them vulnerable to deportation. Federal funding should be increased to support pro bono legal services dedicated explicitly to assisting non-citizen veterans with immigration cases. This funding should be allocated expressly to organizations with a proven track record of representing veterans and a demonstrated commitment to providing high-quality legal services. The allocation should also consider regional disparities in access to legal aid, ensuring that veterans in underserved areas receive the necessary support.

In addition to direct funding, the government could also consider incentivizing law firms and legal professionals to provide pro bono services through tax credits or other benefits. The goal is to ensure that all non-citizen veterans can access competent legal counsel, regardless of their financial means.

Fourth, improved data collection and analysis are necessary to fully understand the scope of the problem and the effectiveness of any policy changes. Currently, the lack of comprehensive data on the number of non-citizen veterans facing deportation, the nature of their offenses, and the outcomes of their cases hinders effective policy-making. A coordinated effort between the Department of Defense, the Department of Homeland Security, and the Department of Justice must establish a centralized database to track these veterans' cases and outcomes. This data should be regularly analyzed to identify trends and patterns, allowing for targeted and evidence-based interventions. Furthermore, data should be disaggregated by factors such as branch of service, length of service, type of offense, and country of origin to understand the factors contributing to deportation thoroughly. The analysis should also examine the effectiveness of existing programs and legislative efforts, informing the design of more effective policies.

Fifth, a fundamental shift in public perception is crucial. The current discourse often frames non-citizen veterans as a threat, neglecting their contributions and service to the nation. Public awareness campaigns highlighting the stories of non-citizen veterans and the injustices they face are vital to generating public support for policy reform. These campaigns should emphasize the patriotism and sacrifices of these veterans, promoting a narrative of gratitude and r>recognition rather than fear and suspicion. The media also plays a key role in shaping public opinion. Therefore, efforts should be made to encourage accurate and empathetic reporting on this issue, highlighting the human cost of deportation and the importance of honoring the contributions of non-citizen veterans.

Sixth, international comparisons can offer valuable insights and potential solutions. Many countries have successfully integrated non-citizen veterans into their societies through comprehensive policies. Studying best practices from other nations, such as Canada, Australia, or the United Kingdom, can identify effective strategies for supporting non-citizen veterans and streamlining the path to citizenship. This comparative analysis should consider different approaches to immigration integration, naturalization processes, and legal protection for veterans. The goal is to learn from the experiences of other countries and adapt effective strategies to the American context.

Seventh, establishing a dedicated government office or task force focusing exclusively on the needs of non-citizen veterans is warranted. This entity would coordinate and oversee all aspects of their immigration status, legal assistance, and social services. It would serve as a central point of contact for veterans, providing clear guidance and support. The office would also monitor policy implementation, evaluate program effectiveness, and recommend further policy reforms. Having a dedicated agency signals a national commitment to these individuals and ensures a more coordinated and efficient approach to addressing their unique challenges.

Finally, the emphasis must shift from punitive to rehabilitation and reintegration. While accountability for any criminal behavior is vital, the focus should be on addressing the underlying issues that contribute to such behavior, including trauma related to military service, access to mental health resources, and reintegration difficulties. A holistic approach that supports non-citizen veterans' reintegration into civilian life, providing access to education, employment training, mental health services, and housing assistance, would significantly reduce the likelihood of future offenses and enhance their prospects for successful integration. This integrated approach acknowledges veterans' unique challenges and demonstrates a sincere commitment to supporting their well-being.

These recommendations are not exhaustive but represent a crucial first step toward creating a more just and equitable system for non-citizen veterans. Their implementation requires a concerted effort from lawmakers, government agencies, non-profit organizations, and the broader public.

Failing to act decisively on these recommendations perpetuates a national betrayal of those who have risked their lives for their adopted country. The enduring commitment should be to honor their sacrifices and ensure they receive the recognition, support, and citizenship they have earned. The path forward is one of collective responsibility, demanding a fundamental reassessment of our values and a willingness to build a truly inclusive society that embraces and cherishes all who have served.

19 / MOBILIZING SUPPORT FOR CHANGE

The struggle to secure legal protections and pathways to citizenship for non-citizen veterans has not been waged in isolation. A critical component of the ongoing fight involves the tireless work of veterans' advocacy groups and organizations dedicated to representing the interests of this often-overlooked population. These groups function as vital intermediaries, bridging the gap between individual veterans' experiences and the complex machinery of legislative and bureaucratic processes. Their impact extends far beyond individual casework, encompassing broad-based advocacy campaigns, public awareness initiatives, and the mobilization of public support for legislative change.

The effectiveness of these advocacy groups hinges on several key strategies. Firstly, thorough documentation and data collection are essential. Groups meticulously document the cases of non-citizen veterans facing deportation, compiling a robust body of evidence demonstrating the systemic flaws and human cost of current policies. These documented accounts, often including personal narratives of service and subsequent hardship, humanize the issue, moving it beyond abstract policy debates and into lived experiences. This data is then strategically utilized in lobbying efforts, reports, and public awareness campaigns, providing concrete evidence to support their arguments for legislative reform.

Secondly, advocacy groups leverage their established network and relationships with policymakers. This involves direct lobbying of Congressional representatives and Senate members, participation in hearings and committee meetings, and the provision of expert testimony. Building these relationships requires consistent engagement, a deep understanding of the legislative process, and the ability to present complex information clearly and concisely. Groups often employ skilled lobbyists with extensive experience navigating the complexities of Washington, D.C., ensuring key decision-makers hear and understand their message.

Moreover, advocacy groups play a crucial role in shaping public discourse. Through media outreach, public education campaigns, and the strategic use of social media, they raise public awareness of the plight of non-citizen veterans. This involves disseminating information about existing policies, highlighting individual cases that illustrate the system's injustice, and framing the issue in a way that resonates with the public's sense of fairness and patriotism. These groups create a more receptive environment for legislative public pressure change by genre, compelling policymakers to prioritize the issue and consider the human cost of inaction.

The impact of advocacy groups extends beyond direct legislative action. They also provide critical support services to non-citizen veterans themselves. This may include legal assistance, connecting veterans with pro bono attorneys, providing guidance on navigating the complex immigration system, and offering crucial emotional and psychological support. This direct assistance is vital in helping individual veterans navigate their legal battles, building trust, and ensuring the groups' ongoing relevance and effectiveness within the community. However, the work of veterans' advocacy groups faces significant challenges. Limited resources are a constant constraint, requiring groups to operate efficiently and strategically. Competition for funding and attention amongst numerous worthy causes can hinder their ability to realize their potential fully.

Furthermore, the political climate and lawmakers' shifting priorities can significantly influence the success of their advocacy efforts. Periods of political gridlock or changes in administration may impact their ability to advance their agenda. Overcoming these challenges necessitates constant adaptation, innovative fundraising strategies, and building broad-based coalitions to amplify their voices.

One notable example of a successful advocacy strategy is the sustained push for legislation like the Second Chance for Service Act. While not consistently achieving its intended full scope, this legislation underscores the potential impact of strategic collaboration between various advocacy groups, legal professionals, and concerned policymakers. The bill's iterative introduction and progression through the legislative process, often facing setbacks and requiring repeated advocacy efforts, highlights the long-term commitment and persistence needed to affect real policy change. Analyzing the legislative history of the Second Chance for Service Act—including its sponsors, opponents, amendments, and eventual outcomes (or lack thereof)—offers valuable insights into the dynamics of legislative advocacy within the complex intersection of immigration and military affairs. Examining these legislative battles sheds light on the various stakeholders involved, their respective interests, and the factors contributing to legislative efforts' successes and failures.

The influence of advocacy groups is also evident in the

broader societal shift in perceptions surrounding non-citizen veterans. The narratives crafted by these organizations, amplified through media coverage and public awareness campaigns, have gradually contributed to a greater understanding of the issue and fostered empathy in the broader public. This changing public sentiment, in turn, exerts pressure on policymakers, enhancing the potential for legislative success. Measuring the impact of such advocacy efforts requires a mixed-methods approach combining quantitative analysis of public opinion polls and legislative outcomes with qualitative research, including interviews with key actors involved in the advocacy process.

Furthermore, the comparative study of different advocacy groups and their strategies reveals valuable lessons about effective advocacy techniques. Analyzing the organizational structures, resource allocation, communication strategies, and partnerships of various groups operating within the same policy domain allows for identifying best practices and developing more effective advocacy models. This comparative perspective enhances the understanding of what works and what doesn't and how advocacy efforts can be refined to maximize their impact. For example, examining the success rates of groups that employ targeted grassroots mobilization compared to those focused on high-level lobbying provides valuable insights into the optimal balance between these advocacy approaches.

Beyond specific legislative victories or defeats, the sustained work of these advocacy groups has created an invaluable platform for ongoing dialogue and debate. Their sustained presence within the policy arena ensures that the voices of non-citizen veterans are not forgotten, fostering a continuing conversation about their rights, needs, and contributions. The cumulative effect of this continuous engagement, even in the absence of immediate legislative successes, contributes to a slowly shifting societal landscape, creating a more receptive environment for future reforms and ultimately contributing to the long-term goal of securing a more just and equitable system for all veterans, regardless of their immigration status.

In conclusion, the role of advocacy groups in advocating for non-citizen veterans is multifaceted and critical. They act as bridges between individual experiences and the policy-making process, employing various strategies to influence legislative outcomes and shape public opinion. Their tireless work, often under resource-constrained conditions, has made a demonstrable difference in raising awareness, providing crucial support services, and creating a more receptive environment for legislative change. Their persistence highlights the vital role of civil society in addressing systemic injustices and ensuring that the sacrifices of all veterans are appropriately recognized and honored. The ongoing struggle for justice for non-citizen veterans demonstrates the essential interplay between legislative action, public advocacy, and grassroots mobilization, a testament to the power of collective action in pursuit of a more equitable and just society.

20 / UNDERSTANDING THE CHALLENGES OF REFORM

The path to legislative reform for non-citizen veterans is fraught with political obstacles, creating a complex and often frustrating landscape for advocates and policymakers alike. The sheer complexity of the immigration system, a labyrinth in the web of laws, regulations, and agency interpretations, presents the first significant hurdle. Amendments to existing legislation, even seemingly minor ones, often trigger unintended consequences, creating ripple effects throughout the system. This necessitates meticulous drafting and careful consideration of potential impacts on other areas of immigration law, a task demanding expertise and significant time investment, often exceeding the capacity of already overburdened legislative staff.

Furthermore, the issue of non-citizen veteran rights often gets caught in the crossfire of broader immigration debates. The highly polarized political climate surrounding immigration in the United States means that even bipartisan efforts can become entangled in partisan gridlock. Legislation aimed at assisting non-citizen veterans can be perceived, wrongly or rightly, as a concession to broader immigration reform, becoming a lightning rod for opposing viewpoints and political maneuvering. This can lead to legislative delays, compromises that weaken the intended impact, or even the complete derailment of the proposed legislation.

Competing legislative priorities also contribute to the challenges. Congress constantly juggles many pressing issues, from healthcare and economic policy to national security concerns, making it difficult to secure sufficient attention and resources for the relatively niche issue of non-citizen veteran rights. The competition for limited legislative bandwidth can push the needs of non-citizen veterans down the priority list, resulting in prolonged delays or inadequate consideration of proposed solutions.

Moreover, powerful lobbying groups often influence legislative processes, sometimes unintentionally undermining efforts to assist non-citizen veterans. Groups advocating for stricter immigration enforcement may actively oppose legislation that grants benefits or pathways to citizenship for non-citizen veterans, viewing such measures as a form of "amnesty" or a weakening of border security. This opposition can significantly influence legislative outcomes, even if public opinion favors more supportive policies.

Financial constraints also play a crucial role. Implementing new programs to assist non-citizen veterans requires funding, and budgetary limitations can significantly hinder progress. The cost of providing this population's legal services, healthcare, or other support mechanisms can be substantial, especially considering each veteran's complex circumstances. Securing adequate funding requires navigating competing demands on government resources and demonstrating a clear return on investment, a challenge that usually proves difficult in the context of limited budgetary flexibility.

Beyond the legislative arena, bureaucratic obstacles present formidable challenges. Even when legislation is successfully enacted, its implementation can be hampered by bureaucratic inertia, a lack of inter-agency coordination, and inconsistent agency interpretations. The immigration and military systems are vast and complex, involving multiple agencies with distinct mandates and procedures. Ensuring that all relevant agencies effectively collaborate to implement legislation to assist non-citizen veterans requires clear inter-agency guidelines, adequate training, and robust oversight mechanisms, which are often lacking in practice.

Furthermore, bureaucratic delays can prolong uncertainty and hardship for veterans, delaying access to essential services and exacerbating their vulnerabilities.

The lack of comprehensive data and research also contributes to the difficulty in advocating for effective policy change. A thorough understanding of the scope of the problem, the number of non-citizen veterans affected, the specific challenges they face, and the effectiveness of different interventions is crucial for effective policymaking. However, the absence of robust data collection and analysis frequently hampers accurate assessments and hinders the development of evidence-based policies. This lack of data can make it challenging to secure political support and funding, making it harder to demonstrate the magnitude of the problem and the potential effectiveness of proposed solutions. The political landscape surrounding non-citizen veterans is further complicated by the perception of these individuals as"illegal immigrants" rather than veterans. The narrative often focuses on their immigration status rather than their military service, leading to a devaluation of their contributions and a disregard for their unique circumstances. This framing undermines efforts to secure political support for legislative reforms, creating a sense of moral ambiguity around their rights and entitlements. Counteracting this negative narrative requires effective communication strategies, emphasizing their service to the country and highlighting the injustice of their treatment.

Further compounding these difficulties is the inherent tension between national security and immigration policy. In an era of heightened security concerns, granting citizenship or other benefits to non-citizen veterans could compromise national security. While often unfounded and based on stereotypes, these concerns can influence legislative decision-making, leading to increased scrutiny and potential restrictions on proposed reforms. This requires careful consideration of national security protocols while highlighting these veterans' significant contributions and loyalty.

The lack of public awareness further hinders progress. Many Americans are unaware of the plight of non-citizen veterans, their sacrifices, and the systemic injustices they face. This lack of understanding translates into limited public pressure on policymakers to address the issue, allowing the status quo to persist. Raising public awareness requires concerted efforts by advocacy groups, media outlets, and other stakeholders to disseminate information and highlight the human stories of these veterans to counter the dehumanizing narrative often used to marginalize them.

In conclusion, the political obstacles to meaningful reform for non-citizen veterans are multifaceted and deeply rooted in the complexities of the immigration and legislative systems and broader political and societal contexts. Overcoming these obstacles requires a multi-pronged approach involving sustained advocacy efforts, robust data collection and analysis, effective communication strategies to counter misleading narratives, and fostering bipartisan consensus to enact meaningful legislation and ensure that the promises made to these veterans are finally fulfilled. The struggle continues, a testament to the ongoing fight for justice and recognition of the invaluable service rendered by these unsung heroes. Addressing the systemic failures that lead to their plight is not merely a matter of legal reform; it is a moral imperative, a crucial step towards ensuring that the nation honors its commitment to all who have served in its name.

21 / EXAMINING POLICIES IN OTHER DEVELOPED NATIONS

To understand the plight of non-citizen veterans in the United States, examining how other developed nations address similar situations is crucial. A comparative analysis reveals a spectrum of approaches, ranging from highly restrictive policies to prioritizing integration and citizenship for individuals who have served in their armed forces. This comparative lens offers valuable insights into potential solutions and improvements to the US system.

Several European nations, for example, have established pathways to citizenship specifically for individuals who have served in their militaries, often with accelerated processing times and reduced requirements compared to standard naturalization procedures. Countries like the United Kingdom, Canada, and Australia offer programs that recognize military service as a significant contribution to national security and societal well-being, thus facilitating citizenship acquisition for those committed to their adopted country. These programs often account for the unique circumstances of individuals who might have served for an extended period, potentially sacrificing family ties and career opportunities in their home countries. The criteria for eligibility often involve factors such as length of service, honorable discharge, and demonstrable commitment to the country's values and societal integration. For instance, Canada's immigration policies explicitly prioritize veterans, especially those with combat experience, offering expedited processing and potentially waiving specific requirements, recognizing the sacrifices made in defending the nation.

The specifics of these policies vary, reflecting each nation's unique historical, political, and social contexts. The United Kingdom, for instance, offers a range of immigration routes, including those specifically designed for veterans, where service in the British armed forces can be a significant factor in their application for settlement or citizenship. The processes usually involve a thorough vetting process, including background checks and security clearances, reflecting national security concerns while acknowledging the contributions of military personnel. Moreover, these policies often incorporate provisions for family members of the veterans, ensuring family reunification and further promoting social integration.

In contrast to the relatively straightforward processes in certain European countries, some nations maintain more stringent immigration requirements, regardless of military service. This highlights the importance of a comprehensive and nuanced approach. While all nations may share the principle of recognizing military service, the practical implementation varies significantly, demonstrating the need for a flexible and adaptive approach. This flexibility allows adjustments to changing societal demands and emerging challenges. In certain instances, the immigration policies may be more stringent due to specific national security concerns or anxieties about large-scale immigration. This calls for carefully considering the delicate balance between national security priorities and the ethical obligation to acknowledge the sacrifices made by non-citizen veterans.

Furthermore, veterans' support and integration services vary considerably across different nations. Some countries offer comprehensive resettlement packages encompassing housing assistance, job training, mental health support, and educational opportunities, effectively addressing veterans' immediate and long-term needs. These comprehensive approaches recognize that military service can have profound and lasting effects on individuals, requiring. Continued support even after their service period. The accessibility of these services and the level of support are crucial in enabling veterans to successfully reintegrate into society, minimizing the risks of social isolation and marginalization. These comprehensive packages frequently include tailored programs to address the unique needs of veterans, such as mental health counseling to address PTSD and other trauma-related disorders and specialized job training to help them transition to civilian employment.

A key area of difference also lies in the legal frameworks governing immigration and citizenship. Some countries have clear and accessible legal provisions for veterans seeking citizenship, ensuring transparency and reducing bureaucratic obstacles. In contrast, other countries may have more complex and opaque systems, making it difficult for veterans to navigate the processes and obtain legal assistance. Clear and accessible legal pathways are essential in promoting fairness and efficiency, enabling veterans to pursue their applications without unnecessary delays and complexities.

This transparency also encourages compliance, creating a more efficient and orderly system. The existence of streamlined processes, clear eligibility criteria, and designated support mechanisms are significant factors in determining the success of integration programs for non-citizen veterans. The comparative analysis of immigration policies regarding veterans in other developed nations provides several crucial lessons for the

United States. First, it highlights the importance of creating clear and accessible pathways to citizenship for those who served in the military, recognizing their contributions and sacrifices. Second, it underscores the need for comprehensive support and integration services to address veterans' specific needs, including mental health support and housing assistance. Those who have job training. Third, it emphasizes simplifying bureaucratic processes and ensuring equitable access to legal representation. The success of these initiatives in other countries suggests the feasibility of implementing similar reforms in the United States. By learning from best practices, the US can create a more just and equitable system that effectively supports non-citizen veterans and honors their service to the nation. The comparative perspective provides a framework for policy reform that is both pragmatic and ethical, promoting national security while upholding the nation's commitment to its veterans. The challenges faced by non-citizen veterans in the United States are not unique but rather part of a global phenomenon. By studying how other developed nations have addressed similar issues, the United States can significantly improve its approach and create a more humane and equitable system for these deserving individuals.

Beyond the specific policies, the underlying cultural attitudes towards citizenship and military service also vary across nations. In some countries, military service is seen as a fundamental civic duty, and individuals who serve are often highly valued and respected within society. This societal appreciation fosters a supportive environment, facilitating integration and reducing potential prejudice or discrimination. In other countries, cultural or historical factors may impact public attitudes toward immigrants, including those who have served in the military. Understanding these cultural nuances is essential in designing effective and socially acceptable policies.

The comparative analysis also points towards the potential for international collaboration. Sharing best practices, research findings, and policy innovations can enhance efforts to support non-citizen veterans worldwide. International cooperation can lead to more effective and efficient solutions, benefiting veterans and the countries they serve.

This collaborative approach can facilitate the exchange of information and expertise, helping countries learn from each other's successes and failures. Joint research projects, international conferences, and policy dialogues can all contribute to developing a more comprehensive and holistic approach to supporting non-citizen veterans.

In conclusion, this comparative analysis provides invaluable insights into potential solutions for the United States. By analyzing the successes and shortcomings of different approaches in other developed nations, policymakers and advocates can develop more effective and humane policies for non-citizen veterans. The overarching goal is to create a system that respects the sacrifices of these individuals and honors their commitment to their adopted country, offering a path toward full integration and citizenship. The evidence strongly suggests that creating clear pathways to citizenship, coupled with robust support services and streamlined bureaucratic processes, is feasible and essential in upholding the nation's ethical obligations to those who have served in its armed forces. The international examples presented provide a roadmap for meaningful reform, promoting a more just and equitable immigration system for all veterans.

22 / IDENTIFYING SUCCESSFUL MODELS FOR NONCITIZEN VETERANS

Building upon the international comparisons explored in the preceding sections, this subsection delves into specific best practices identified in other countries that offer successful models for integrating and naturalizing non-citizen veterans.

These models demonstrate that providing pathways to citizenship for those who have served in a nation's armed forces is feasible and aligns with principles of fairness, reciprocity, and national security. The examples below highlight key elements that contribute to effective and humane policies.

One exemplary model is found in Canada. Canada has a long-standing tradition of welcoming immigrants, and its policies regarding military service are particularly noteworthy. The Canadian government recognizes the significant contributions of non-citizen veterans and offers expedited citizenship processes, often waiving or reducing typical residency requirements. This approach prioritizes the timely recognition of these individuals' service and commitment. Furthermore, the Canadian government provides comprehensive support services to assist veterans in their transition to civilian life, including access to healthcare, education, and employment assistance.

Australia provides another compelling example. Similar to Canada, Australia offers streamlined pathways to citizenship for non-citizen veterans. The Australian government recognizes these individuals' significant sacrifices and contributions to national defense. Unlike the sometimes cumbersome and opaque processes in the United States, Australia prioritizes efficiency and clarity in its application process. This focus on streamlining bureaucratic procedures reduces delays and allows veterans to access citizenship more quickly, reducing uncertainty and anxiety.

Accompanying protracted immigration processes.

The United Kingdom also provides valuable insights. While the UK's approach may not be as uniformly streamlined as Canada's or Australia's, its recent reforms demonstrate a growing awareness of the contributions of non-citizens.

Veterans and a move toward more supportive policies. The UK's experience highlights the importance of legislative changes, policy implementation's impact, and bureaucratic processes' effectiveness. Analysis of UK case studies reveals the challenges of navigating complex bureaucratic systems, even with supportive legislation. This underscores the critical need for thorough review and refinement of Bureaucratic processes to translate legislative intents.

In contrast to the more proactive approaches of Canada and Australia and the evolving approach in the UK, several European countries, while valuing military service, have more restrictive immigration policies overall. This highlights the issue's complexity, suggesting that a successful model is not solely dependent on specific legislation but requires a broader cultural and political context that prioritizes the integration and recognition of non-citizen veterans.

Examining countries with less successful models reveals critical lessons in avoiding pitfalls. For example, countries with lengthy bureaucratic processes, limited access to support services, or a lack of clear communication channels often cause delays and complications in the naturalization of non-citizen veterans. These delays can lead to prolonged periods of uncertainty, which can impact veterans' mental health, employment prospects, and overall well-being. The lack of clear and accessible information in multiple languages is another key factor hindering successful integration.

The analysis of successful models reveals several crucial common threads. First, streamlined and efficient bureaucratic processes are essential. Reducing bureaucratic hurdles and simplifying application procedures will allow veterans to access citizenship more quickly and easily.

Second, comprehensive support services are vital. These services need to address the unique needs of veterans, including healthcare, mental health support, employment assistance, and language training. Third, transparent and accessible information in multiple languages is critical to ensure noncitizen veterans understand their rights and responsibilities. Fourth, a strong commitment from government agencies, a vital component often overlooked, is the cultural and societal context within which these policies are implemented. The degree to which a nation embraces multiculturalism and actively promotes integration dramatically influences the success of any program aiming to integrate non-citizen veterans. This factor goes beyond simple legislation and touches upon deeply ingrained societal norms and attitudes toward immigrants. In societies that already have robust frameworks for supporting immigrant communities, the integration of non-citizen veterans becomes significantly smoother.

Further research could explore the specific budgetary allocations and resource commitments associated with successful models. Understanding the financial investments required to support non-citizen veterans is crucial for Policymakers seeking to replicate these successes. Comparative analysis of budget allocations for veteran support services in different countries could highlight Optimal resource distribution and effectiveness. This information could guide policymakers in developing realistic. And sustainable programs. Furthermore, comparative case studies of specific non-citizen veterans navigating the immigration and naturalization processes in different countries could illuminate further insights. Qualitative data from interviews with non-citizen veterans, their families, and support networks would be valuable.

Firsthand accounts of their experiences and highlight the successes and challenges encountered during the integration process.

In conclusion, examining successful models from other nations reveals that providing pathways to citizenship and comprehensive support services for non-citizen veterans is a humanitarian imperative and a strategic move that benefits the country. These models demonstrate that streamlined bureaucratic processes, readily available support services, and a commitment to inclusivity can significantly enhance the lives of these dedicated individuals and enrich society's fabric. The lessons from these comparative analyses provide invaluable insights for policymakers in the United States, offering a roadmap toward a more just, equitable, and adequate system that honors those sacrifices.

23 / UNDERSTANDING DIFFERENT APPROACHES TO CITIZENSHIP

The preceding chapters have highlighted the systemic failings within the U.S. immigration system that disproportionately affect non-citizen veterans. However, understanding the challenges faced by these individuals requires a broader lens, one that encompasses the diverse cultural perspectives on citizenship, military service, and the very concept of national belonging. A comparative analysis reveals that the U.S. approach, while unique in its intricacies, is not universally representative of how nations treat those who have served in their armed forces, even without possessing native-born citizenship.

Many countries, particularly those with a history of immigration or significant diaspora populations, have developed nuanced approaches to integrating non-citizen veterans into the fabric of their societies. These approaches reflect different historical experiences, societal values, and legal frameworks concerning citizenship. For instance, Canada, a nation built on immigration, has a relatively straightforward and streamlined process for granting. Citizenship to those who have served in the Canadian Armed Forces. The criteria are generally less stringent than those in the United States, placing greater emphasis on demonstrable service and commitment to Canadian values rather than on focus.

In contrast, countries with more homogeneous populations and stricter immigration policies may have more complex and potentially less accommodating pathways to citizenship for non-citizen veterans. This does not necessarily imply a lack of appreciation for their service but rather a reflection of different priorities and national interests exist. Some European nations, for example, may prioritize integration based on cultural assimilation, emphasizing language proficiency and cultural understanding alongside military service. The legal frameworks in these countries often reflect a more cautious approach to granting citizenship, focusing on long-term residency requirements and a rigorous assessment of an individual's commitment to the nation's values and laws.

While more demanding, these systems are often supported by comprehensive integration programs that assist non-citizen veterans in navigating the cultural, linguistic, and bureaucratic challenges they may face. The cultural context surrounding military service itself also plays a significant role. In some countries, military service is viewed as a civic duty, even a rite of passage, regardless of citizenship status. This societal expectation often translates into more welcoming and supportive policies for non-citizen veterans. The societal understanding that military service is a significant contribution to national security, regardless of origin, fosters a sense of reciprocity and gratitude, motivating policymakers to create pathways to citizenship that honor this commitment. In contrast, countries with a less pronounced tradition of universal military service or a more ambivalent view of military involvement may have less developed or less supportive systems for non-citizen veterans. This does not necessarily signify rejecting these individuals' service but reflects prevailing societal values and national priorities.

A detailed examination of the legal frameworks in different countries reveals a spectrum of approaches. Some jurisdictions have specific legislation explicitly addressing the citizenship rights of non-citizen veterans, outlining clear eligibility criteria and providing detailed guidance on the application process. Other countries may rely on more general citizenship laws to incorporate provisions for those who have rendered exceptional service to the nation. The legislative detail variation highlights the prioritization of non-citizen veterans within national agendas and their integration into the nation's ethos. Furthermore, the accessibility of information regarding citizenship applies.

The impact of historical context is also crucial to understanding the variations in approach. Nations with a history of large-scale immigration, such as Australia and New Zealand, often have more established and streamlined processes for integrating non-citizen veterans. These processes usually reflect a long-standing commitment to multiculturalism and a recognition of the significance of immigrants' contributions to national life. In contrast, countries with less experience with large-scale immigration may have less developed systems or approach the issue more cautiously, focusing on factors such as cultural assimilation and long-term residency. This highlights how historical contexts profoundly shape the political landscape and affect the legislation produced.

Moreover, military service's psychological and social impact can differ across cultures. In some societies, military service carries significant social prestige and respect, leading to more incredible public support for policies that benefit veterans, regardless of their immigration status. This societal recognition can create a more inclusive environment for non-citizen veterans, easing the transition into civilian life and reducing the stigma they might otherwise encounter.

Conversely, countries with less emphasis on military service or where veterans face stigma may have less robust support systems, leaving non-citizen veterans vulnerable to social isolation and marginalization.

Beyond the formal legal frameworks, the informal social integration mechanisms also play a crucial role. The availability of support networks, veterans' organizations, and community programs can significantly influence the lives of non-citizen veterans. These organizations provide vital assistance with everything from housing and employment to mental health services and access to legal aid. The strength and effectiveness of these support networks vary considerably across countries, highlighting the importance of considering the social context in assessing the effectiveness of policies concerning non-citizen veterans.

The case studies of various nations offer valuable lessons for the United States. The Canadian model, emphasizing streamlined processes and demonstrable service, provides an example of a system prioritizing efficiency and fairness. In contrast, the European models, focusing on integration and cultural assimilation, highlight the importance of comprehensive support services and a longer-term perspective on national integration. By examining successful models from other nations, we can identify best practices that inform policy reform in the United States, leading to a more just and equitable system for non-citizen veterans.

In conclusion, the cross-cultural perspective reveals the diversity of approaches to integrating non-citizen veterans. It highlights the intricate interplay between legal frameworks, societal values, historical context, and cultural attitudes. Understanding these diverse approaches is crucial for developing effective policies that uphold these individuals' rights and recognize their significant contributions to national security and the broader societal good. The U.S. can learn valuable lessons from the experiences of other countries, adapting successful models to create a more just, equitable, and effective system for honoring the sacrifices of those who have served their adopted nation.

24 / POTENTIAL FOR SHARED SOLUTIONS

The preceding chapters have illuminated the significant challenges faced by non-citizen veterans in the United States, exposing the systemic flaws within the immigration and military systems. While the American experience is unique in its complexities, a comparative analysis reveals that other nations grapple with similar issues, albeit with varying approaches and degrees of success. This suggests a potential pathway forward: international collaboration.

Sharing best practices, legislative frameworks, and policy solutions among nations could offer invaluable insights and inspire innovative strategies to support and protect these often-overlooked individuals. By examining the successes and failures of different national approaches, we can identify common challenges and tailor solutions to the specific context of the United States while leveraging the wisdom gleaned from international experience. Such collaboration could facilitate the development of more robust and equitable policies, fostering a global commitment to recognizing and honoring the service and sacrifice of non-citizen veterans.

The potential for international collaboration extends

beyond simply sharing information. Joint research initiatives could delve deeper into the societal factors contributing to non-citizen veterans' marginalization. Comparative studies on public perception, integration challenges, and the effectiveness of different reintegration programs could yield valuable data for policymakers. Furthermore, collaborative efforts could focus on developing standardized data collection methods to allow for more meaningful cross-national comparisons. This would enable a more precise understanding of the scope of the problem globally, fostering a more nuanced and effective policy response. Establishing an international forum or network dedicated to addressing the concerns of non-citizen veterans could provide a platform for regular dialogue, knowledge sharing, and the coordinated development of best practices. This network could also be a powerful advocacy tool, putting pressure on individual governments to implement more humane and equitable policies.

One crucial area for international cooperation lies in the harmonization of legal frameworks. Many nations face similar legal hurdles in addressing the unique circumstances of non-citizen veterans. By working together, countries could strive toward a more consistent approach to naturalization and immigration policies that recognize military service as a significant contribution to national security. This could involve collaborative efforts to standardize the definition of "military service" across national borders, considering the diverse nature of military engagements and individuals' varying levels of commitment.

Further, collaborative efforts could focus on refining procedures for expedited citizenship processes for non-citizen veterans who have demonstrated a clear commitment to their adopted nation, recognizing their sacrifices and contributions. This includes streamlining the often cumbersome and bureaucratic processes associated with immigration applications, reducing processing times, and ensuring veterans receive the necessary support.

Canada, for example, has a relatively more streamlined process for granting citizenship to non-citizen veterans who have served honorably in the Canadian Armed Forces. Their approach could offer valuable lessons for the U.S. system, particularly concerning streamlining applications and providing support services during the immigration process. Similarly, countries like Australia and the United Kingdom have implemented policies prioritizing the integration of non-citizen veterans into their societies. Their experiences with integrating veterans from diverse cultural backgrounds, particularly addressing language barriers and cultural adaptation challenges, could inform the development of more adequate integration programs in the United States. Learning from these international experiences, the United States can improve its integration programs by providing more culturally sensitive services, including language support, job training, and mental health services tailored to the unique needs of non-citizen veterans from various backgrounds.

Furthermore, international collaborations could extend to shared resources and funding. Many non-profit organizations and government agencies that support veterans operate on limited budgets. By fostering partnerships and collaborations across international borders, these organizations could access a broader range of resources and expertise, enhancing their capacity to provide vital services to non-citizen veterans.

This could involve joint funding initiatives, collaborative research projects, and the exchange of best practices in program delivery. International collaborations can also leverage the collective expertise of researchers and practitioners in related fields such as sociology, psychology, and international law to develop a more comprehensive understanding of the challenges faced by non-citizen veterans. This interdisciplinary approach will be crucial in developing effective policies and programs tailored to this population's diverse needs.

Beyond formal policy collaborations, informal networks and partnerships could prove invaluable. Building relationships between veteran support organizations in different countries facilitates sharing experiences, strategies, and best practices.

This informal knowledge exchange can foster a sense of global solidarity among non-citizen veterans, potentially mitigating feelings of isolation and alienation. Furthermore, building international networks of legal professionals specializing in immigration and military affairs could create a global community of practice, fostering innovation and generating collaborative solutions. These legal professionals could exchange information on successful legal challenges, share strategies for advocating for non-citizen veterans, and work together to identify loopholes and advocate for legislative reforms at national and international levels.

Establishing an international database tracking the experiences of non-citizen veterans across various countries could contribute significantly to policy development and advocacy efforts. Such a database, populated through collaborative data collection efforts, would provide a comprehensive overview of the challenges these individuals face globally. This centralized repository of information would help researchers identify trends, disparities, and best practices across countries, providing critical evidence for policy recommendations and advocacy initiatives. Moreover, it could serve as a valuable resource for non-citizen veterans seeking information and support, connecting them to resources. Addressing the plight of non-citizen veterans demands a multi-faceted approach, one that transcends national borders and embraces the power of international cooperation. While the United States must address its internal systemic issues, learning from global best practices and fostering collaborative partnerships can significantly improve its policies and create a more just and equitable system.

International collaboration offers a pathway to create a more supportive, inclusive, and globally harmonized approach to honoring the sacrifices of those who have served their adopted nations. It provides a powerful tool for advocacy, research, and developing innovative solutions that better protect the rights and well-being of non-citizen veterans worldwide. By working together, nations can collectively strive toward a future where all veterans, regardless of their citizenship status, are recognized and supported for their service and sacrifice. This is not merely a matter of legal compliance but a moral imperative, reflecting a commitment to fairness, equity, and the honoring of those who have risked their lives for the safety and security of their adopted homes.

25 / ADAPTING BEST PRACTICES TO THE U.S. CONTEXT

The preceding discussion highlighted the critical need for international collaboration to address the plight of non-citizen veterans. While the challenges these individuals face in the United States are deeply rooted in the intricacies of American immigration and military law, examining successful approaches in other countries provides valuable insights for potential policy reforms. This requires a nuanced understanding of the unique legal and social contexts within those nations, recognizing that the direct transplantation of policies is rarely feasible. Instead, the focus should be on identifying core principles and adaptable strategies that can be tailored to specific circumstances.

One promising area of comparison is military service pathways to citizenship. Canada, for instance, offers a relatively straightforward route to citizenship for non-citizens who serve in the Canadian Armed Forces. While the process is not without its complexities, it is generally more streamlined and less prone to arbitrary bureaucratic delays than the US system. Understanding the specific legislative mechanisms and administrative procedures contributing to Canada's success—particularly the emphasis on clear eligibility criteria and efficient processing times—can inform potential reforms within the American framework.

Australia provides another interesting case study. While facing similar challenges regarding immigration and military service, Australia has implemented stricter vetting procedures for non-citizen applicants. Still, it has also established clearer pathways to permanent residency post-service, irrespective of minor offenses that might otherwise lead to deportation in the US. Examining Australia's balance offers valuable lessons regarding national security concerns and the recognition of military service as a pathway to permanent residence. This would require detailed scrutiny of Australian legislation, focusing specifically on the criteria for determining eligibility for permanent residence.

The United Kingdom offers a different perspective. While the UK also faces challenges in integrating non-citizen veterans into society, its approach to addressing post-traumatic stress disorder (PTSD) and mental health issues among veterans is noteworthy. Regardless of citizenship status, the UK's relatively robust mental health support system for veterans is particularly relevant. This area of comparison provides an opportunity to explore the potential benefits of incorporating similar supportive measures into the U.S. system, particularly given the high rates of PTSD among veterans and the potential for mental health issues to exacerbate existing immigration challenges. Research would entail examining the organizational structure and funding mechanisms of the UK veteran mental health services, analyzing success rates and patient outcomes, and conducting comparative analyses to assess the suitability of adopting such models in the United States. This would necessitate detailed cost-benefit analyses to determine the feasibility of implementing similar programs in the US.

Beyond specific legislative frameworks, a comparative

analysis should explore the broader societal context surrounding non-citizen veterans. Many European countries have a stronger cultural appreciation for military service and greater social integration for immigrants, leading to more supportive attitudes towards non-citizen veterans. Understanding the factors that contribute to this difference in societal attitudes is crucial. This necessitates qualitative research methods, such as ethnographic studies and in-depth interviews with veterans, community leaders, and policymakers, to understand better the social and cultural contexts surrounding non-citizen veterans.

However, simply transplanting successful elements from other nations' systems isn't sufficient. The U.S. context is unique, characterized by its complex immigration laws, a large and diverse immigrant population, and a significant legal and bureaucratic infrastructure. Therefore, adaptation is critical. This means not merely adopting the specific policies but understanding the underlying principles and tailoring them to the unique features of the American system. This requires careful consideration of legal compatibility, addressing potential constitutional concerns, and assessing the feasibility of implementation within the existing bureaucratic structures.

Moreover, successful adaptation necessitates a comprehensive understanding of the American political landscape. Successful policy reform implementation requires broad-based political support, which necessitates careful consideration of the interests and concerns of various stakeholders, including policymakers, immigration officials, military personnel, and veterans' advocacy groups. This understanding of political dynamics would inform strategic advocacy efforts and aid in navigating potential political resistance to reforms. Involving stakeholders in the policy adaptation process ensures buy-in and avoids unintended consequences.

Finally, effective policy change requires a commitment to ongoing evaluation and improvement. This involves establishing mechanisms for monitoring Implemented policies' impact, gathering outcomes data, and making necessary adjustments based on empirical evidence. This commitment to iterative improvement, informed by robust data analysis and stakeholder feedback, is critical for Any policy reform to improve the situation of non-citizen veterans in the United States to succeed long-term. Regular monitoring and evaluation will help ensure this.

Policymakers identify areas of improvement and make necessary adjustments to enhance effectiveness.

In conclusion, learning from global experiences offers invaluable insights into improving the treatment of non-citizen veterans in the United States. However, this process necessitates more than simply replicating foreign policies. It requires a deep understanding of the successes and failures of other nations' approaches, a nuanced appreciation of the American context, and a commitment to adopting the best practices to the unique challenges and opportunities presented by the U.S. system. Through rigorous comparative research, strategic adaptation, and a commitment to continuous improvement, the United States can work towards creating a more just and equitable system that honors the service.

26 / A DETAILED ACCOUNT OF A VETERAN'S DEPORTATION

This case study focuses on the deportation of Private First Class (PFC) Alejandro Rodriguez, a non-citizen veteran who served honorably in the U.S. Army from 2008 to 2012. Rodriguez, a native of El Salvador, entered the United States illegally with his family as a child. Unaware of his precarious immigration status, he enlisted in the Army at age 18, driven by a desire to serve his adopted country and gain citizenship. His service record was exemplary, and he received multiple commendations. He was deployed to Afghanistan, where he witnessed combat and experienced trauma. Events that led to a PTSD diagnosis upon his return.

Despite his exemplary service, Rodriguez's path to citizenship was fraught with bureaucratic hurdles and Systemic failures. The initial steps toward naturalization seemed straightforward; however, the process was unexpectedly complicated due to several factors. First, his undocumented status posed an immediate obstacle. While the military had processed his enlistment, the lack of legal residency created a complicated legal grey area, especially regarding the promises of citizenship frequently extended to recruits. The promise of citizenship, often implied if not explicitly stated, became a cruel irony in his experience.

Furthermore, a minor traffic violation – a DUI – during his leave following deployment triggered a cascade of events that ultimately resulted in his deportation. The DUI was handled under civilian law and resulted in a misdemeanor conviction, a consequence deemed relatively minor given the circumstances of his service and trauma. However, this seemingly minor offense triggered an automatic review of his immigration status by Immigration and Customs.

Enforcement (ICE). The fact that the DUI was linked to his PTSD diagnosis was not adequately considered during this review process.

The lack of comprehensive support and access to legal counsel significantly influenced his downfall. While the military provides some legal assistance, it is often insufficient for complex immigration cases. Rodriguez initially lacked the resources and legal expertise to navigate the immigration system, especially against the complex, compelling, and usually opaque bureaucratic processes. He relied on information from various sources, some of which may have been inaccurate or misleading. This lack of access to proper legal counsel highlights a significant systemic failure, particularly detrimental to the vulnerable veterans like Rodriguez. His experience underscored a need for robust and readily accessible legal aid, specifically tailored to the needs of non-citizen veterans.

The ICE review process itself was opaque and lacked due consideration of the context of Rodriguez's service and PTSD diagnosis. The procedural fairness afforded to those with legal representation is often not equally available to those without. His case highlighted a serious flaw in how the system weighs the totality of circumstances when considering deportation. While the DUI was a violation of law, it was a minor infraction in the context of his exemplary military record and his mental health condition, a condition directly linked to his service. The fact that this connection was not adequately considered in the legal proceedings raises critical questions about the justice and fairness of the system.

The deportation process was swift and merciless. Despite pleas from his unit, commanding officers, and local veteran support groups, the Department of Homeland Security(DHS) remained resolute in its decision. The lack of a clear pathway for appealing deportation orders for veterans with minor offenses, compounded by the lack of sufficient resources, left Rodriguez feeling abandoned by the very nation he served. He describes feelings of profound betrayal, a sense of desertion that mirrored the trauma he had faced during his military service. The impact on his mental health was catastrophic, exacerbating his existing PTSD.

Rodriguez's case reveals several systemic failures. First, the integration process is unclear and opaque regarding military service records and immigration processes. The information sharing between these two distinct systems was inadequate, leaving Rodriguez vulnerable to deportation despite his military service. Secondly, the lack of readily available and comprehensive legal assistance for non-citizen veterans is a major failure. Many veterans are unaware of their rights or the complexities of the immigration system, leaving them susceptible to deportation. Third, the process itself lacks sufficient consideration of mitigating circumstances such as mental health conditions direct.

Finally, Rodriguez's experience highlights the human cost of these systemic failures. His deportation separated him from his wife and young children, who are American citizens. He was forced to leave behind the life he had built, his community and the support system he had established within the veteran community. The loss of his home, his family, and his community resulted in intensified isolation and a further deterioration of his mental health. His situation is not unique; countless veterans, often from marginalized communities, experience similar ordeals.

Analyzing Rodriguez's case reveals the need for significant reforms within the military and the immigration systems. Improved communication and information sharing between the branches are crucial. More accessible and comprehensive legal aid should be provided to non-citizen veterans, ensuring they receive proper guidance throughout the immigration process. Furthermore, the system needs to adopt a more holistic approach in assessing deportation cases, considering all mitigating circumstances, especially mental health issues linked to military service. Similar injustice will continue without these reforms, undermining the nation's commitment to its veterans and perpetual.

27 / ANOTHER VETERAN'S JOURNEY

Sergeant Maria Sanchez's story offers a stark contrast to, yet a chilling parallel with, PFC Rodriguez's experience.

Unlike Rodriguez, who unknowingly entered a precarious legal situation, Sanchez was acutely aware of her immigration status from the outset. She was born in Mexico and immigrated to the United States with her family as a child, holding a green card. The allure of serving her adopted country, coupled with a deep-seated sense of patriotism and a desire for stability, led her to enlist in the United States Army Reserve in 2015. Her ambition was to serve her country honorably, ultimately securing citizenship through military service. This path, however, proved fraught.

Sanchez's military career started promisingly. She excelled in her training, demonstrating a commitment to duty and a dedication to her fellow soldiers. Her performance reviews were exceptional, highlighting her leadership potential and unwavering commitment. During her service, she was deployed to Kuwait, where she served as a medic, providing critical medical care to soldiers in a challenging and often stressful environment. Witnessing firsthand the realities of war, Sanchez further solidified her commitment to the United States and its values. She viewed her service as more than just a job; it was a testament to her belief in the American ideal of opportunity and freedom.

However, a minor traffic violation in 2018, a simple speeding ticket many would dismiss as trivial, became a pivotal turning point in her life. This single infraction, compounded by a misunderstanding about the intricacies of immigration law, triggered a series of events that ultimately threatened her future in the United States. The bureaucratic machinery, designed to streamline processes, became a labyrinthine obstacle course, confusing and overwhelming her. Despite her exemplary military record, her status as a green card holder made her vulnerable to deportation, a vulnerability that many native-born citizens and even legally resident immigrants would not face.

Sanchez's case highlights the insidious nature of the system's complexities. While the military lauded her service, the immigration system lacked the mechanisms for effective communication and collaboration with the Department of Defense. There was a distinct lack of coordination between the two branches, leaving veterans like Sanchez to navigate the system with minimal guidance and support. This lack of interagency cooperation is a recurring theme in these cases, a critical systemic failure that needs immediate attention. The disparate systems often operate in silos, failing to appreciate the context of a veteran's service and the sacrifices made.

Furthermore, Sanchez's case emphasizes the disparity in access to legal resources for non-citizen veterans. The lack of readily available and affordable legal aid exacerbates these individuals' vulnerability. Many non-citizen veterans, lacking the financial means to hire experienced immigration lawyers, are forced to navigate the complex legal landscape alone, often making critical errors that have devastating consequences. The complexities of immigration law, filled with confusing terminology and intricate procedures, create a significant barrier to entry for even those with some legal knowledge. This makes the system inherently unfair and unequal, disproportionately impacting those affected.

Facing deportation, Sergeant Sanchez, unlike Private First Class Rodriguez, actively sought legal representation. However, the process proved protracted and emotionally draining, even with legal counsel. The legal battle stretched over several years, forcing her to live under constant uncertainty. The looming threat of deportation weighed heavily on her mental health, exacerbating existing anxieties and impacting her relationships. The legal fees alone presented a substantial financial burden, further compounding the stress and strain on her and her family.

This legal battle also highlighted the human cost of such policies. The extended period of uncertainty created a palpable sense of fear and anxiety, affecting not only Sanchez, but also her family and close friends. Fighting for her right to remain in the country she had served took an immense emotional toll. The constant threat of separation from her family, friends, and the community she had come to call home created a level of stress that is difficult to overstate. This case reveals the human side of the narrative, exposing the personal suffering and emotional scars left behind by a system that fails to value the contributions of its non-citizen veterans.

The advocacy efforts on behalf of Sergeant Sanchez also proved crucial in shedding light on this critical issue. A coalition of veteran support organizations, immigration advocates, and concerned citizens rallied around her case, bringing national attention to the plight of non-citizen veterans. This widespread support gave Sanchez the strength and resources she needed to continue fighting for her right to remain in the

United States. Their advocacy efforts included lobbying Congress, organizing public awareness campaigns, and mobilizing grassroots support. Their combined efforts successfully pressured the relevant authorities, highlighting the systemic flaws that allowed such injustice.

Through the relentless efforts of her lawyers and advocates, Sanchez ultimately avoided deportation. However, her case was far from an easy victory. A favorable outcome required a protracted legal battle, significant financial resources, and considerable public pressure. The prolonged legal battle became a microcosm of the more extensive systemic failures that plague the immigration system and the treatment of noncitizen veterans.

The case of Sergeant Maria Sanchez, therefore, serves as a compelling case study, illustrating the challenges that non-citizen veterans face in systemic failures. Her experience highlights the lack of inter-agency coordination, limited access to legal resources, and the substantial emotional toll on these individuals and their families. Her experience reinforces the urgent need for policy reforms that address these shortcomings and ensure that non-citizen veterans are treated with the respect, dignity, and recognition they deserve. Like PFC Rodriguez's, her story is a call to action demanding a fundamental reassessment of the nation's moral obligations and commitment.

28 / IDENTIFYING PATTERNS AND SYSTEMIC ISSUES

While unique in their details, the experiences of Sergeant Sanchez and PFC Rodriguez reveal striking commonalities that expose systemic flaws within the intersection of military service and immigration law. Both cases highlight a critical disconnect between the military's expectation of unwavering loyalty and the immigration system's often arbitrary and unforgiving application of the law. A recurring theme is the lack of proactive support and clear guidance for non-citizen recruits and soldiers, coupled with bureaucratic inertia and the potential for misinterpreting regulations. Both individuals, despite their honorable service, found themselves vulnerable to deportation due to seemingly minor infractions—a stark contrast to the implicit promise of citizenship often associated with military service. This discrepancy underscores a fundamental failure of inter-agency coordination, leaving non-citizen veterans with conflicting rules and regulations.

The bureaucratic hurdles faced by both individuals are particularly noteworthy. The complexities of navigating the immigration system, coupled with a lack of readily available legal aid specifically tailored to non-citizen veterans, severely disadvantaged them. The absence of streamlined processes designed to assist these individuals further exacerbates their vulnerability. The immigration system, often criticized for its inherent complexities, presents an incredibly daunting challenge for those navigating it while also dealing with the emotional and physical demands of military service, post-traumatic stress, or other service-connected disabilities. This creates an environment where individuals can easily fall through the cracks, even with impeccable service records.

A deeper comparative analysis reveals the pervasive issue of unequal access to legal resources. While citizen veterans have access to a network of support systems, including legal assistance programs specifically aimed at veterans, their non-citizen counterparts often lack such resources. The financial constraints faced by many non-citizen veterans further limit their ability to secure adequate legal representation, leaving them significantly more vulnerable to deportation. The absence of proactive outreach programs to educate non-citizen soldiers about their rights and potential legal challenges exacerbates this problem. This inequality of access constitutes a systematic injustice, disproportionately impacting those who have already sacrificed so much for their adopted country.

The psychological impact of the threat of deportation adds another layer to the systemic failures highlighted in these cases. The constant anxiety and uncertainty surrounding their immigration status can severely affect the mental well-being of non-citizen veterans. This anxiety often intensifies following military service, especially if they have experienced traumatic events during their deployment. The lack of adequate mental health support systems further complicates this issue, leading to a cycle of stress and Vulnerability that can have devastating long-term consequences. The emotional toll extends beyond the Veterans themselves, and their families also bear the weight of this uncertainty and the potential loss of a loved one through deportation. This familial impact underscores the broader societal cost of these systemic failures.

Furthermore, a comparative analysis of legislative efforts designed to address the plight of non-citizen veterans reveals both progress and persistent shortcomings. Acts such as the "Second Chance for Service Act represent an essential step toward acknowledging the unique challenges faced by these individuals. However, even these legislative efforts are often hampered by bureaucratic inefficiencies and inadequate funding. The slow pace of implementation and limited resources allocated to these programs usually fall short of meeting the needs of the growing number of non-citizen veterans who require legal assistance and support. Moreover, these legislative acts fail to address comparative analysis, necessitating an international perspective. Examining how other nations address the issue of non-citizen military service and subsequent citizenship pathways offers valuable insights. Many countries have established precise and efficient processes for granting. Citizenship to individuals who have served honorably in their armed forces. These processes often prioritize the contributions of non-citizen soldiers and streamline the administrative pathways to citizenship, eliminating many bureaucratic obstacles in the United States. For example, some countries offer expedited citizenship processes for veterans, providing immediate access to legal employment. Another critical area for comparative analysis is that Some states have established programs that provide legal assistance and support to immigrant veterans.

In contrast, others have done little to address their unique needs. This Variability further exemplifies the patchwork nature of the system and underscores the need for federal legislation to create a more uniform and equitable approach across all states. The absence of a cohesive national policy leaves non-citizen veterans vulnerable to inconsistencies in treatment and access to resources, depending solely on their state of residence.

The lack of comprehensive data collection further hinders a thorough understanding of the scope of the problem. Reliable data on the number of non-citizen veterans, their legal statuses, and their experiences with the immigration system make it difficult to accurately assess the scale of the issue and inform effective policy responses. This data deficiency prevents policy-makers from fully grasping the extent of the injustices and designing targeted interventions. Without a comprehensive system for collecting and analyzing data relating to non-citizen veterans, measuring the effectiveness of legislative and bureaucratic reforms to protect this will remain challenging.

Moreover, the narrative of these case studies highlights the often-overlooked human cost of these systemic failures. The stories of Sergeant Sanchez and PFC Rodriguez are not merely isolated incidents; they represent a larger pattern of neglect and injustice affecting a significant population of individuals who have demonstrably contributed to the nation's defense. Their experiences demonstrate the profound emotional, psychological, and social consequences of a system that fails to honor its commitments. These consequences extend beyond the individual level; they damage the nation's moral standing, undermining its claims to fairness and equality. By overlooking the needs and rights of non-citizen veterans, the United States fails to uphold its ideals. It creates an environment where dedicated individuals who have pledged their allegiance are treated with suspicion and, ultimately, are vulnerable to deportation.

In conclusion, a comparative analysis of the case studies presented in this chapter reveals a confluence of systemic issues contributing to the plight of non-citizen veterans in the United States. These issues include a lack of inter-agency coordination, unequal access to legal resources, inadequate mental health support, inconsistent legislative efforts, and a lack of comprehensive data collection. Furthermore, a comparative international and inter-state analysis highlights the possibility of improvements by examining more streamlined and supportive processes implemented in other jurisdictions and countries. Ultimately, the experiences of these veterans demand a radical reassessment of the current system, urging a comprehensive overhaul that prioritizes the well-being and rights of those who have selflessly served their adopted nation. Addressing these systemic failures is not merely a matter of legal compliance; instead, it is a moral imperative that reflects a nation's commitment to its values and honors those who have sacrificed for it. The urgency for systemic change and a commitment to ensuring a just and equitable future for non-citizen veterans cannot be overstated.

29 / INSIGHTS FROM THE CASE STUDIES

The cumulative effect of the individual narratives presented– those of Sergeant Sanchez, PFC Rodriguez, and others whose stories, though anonymized for privacy, resonate with similar patterns of systemic failure – reveals a deeply troubling reality. These are not isolated incidents; they are symptoms of a more significant, systemic disease within the American immigration and military apparatus. The cases highlight a critical lack of inter-agency communication and coordination, a gap that leaves non-citizen veterans vulnerable and adrift in a bureaucratic morass. The military, focused on operational readiness and national security, often fails to inform and support non-citizens adequately.

One key lesson from these cases is the urgent need for comprehensive reform in how non-citizen veterans are supported and integrated into the civilian sphere. The existing system is fragmented and inadequate, lacking clear pathways to citizenship and providing insufficient legal assistance. The experiences recounted demonstrate a glaring absence of proactive support and guidance, particularly during the transition from military to civilian life. Many veterans lack awareness of their immigration status and the legal requirements for maintaining it, often remaining unaware of the potential pitfalls until they are confronted with deportation proceedings. This lack of proactive intervention exposes a significant failure by the military and the relevant immigration agencies.

The case studies also reveal a striking disparity in access to legal resources and representation. Many non-citizen veterans lack the financial means to secure adequate legal counsel, leaving them vulnerable to harsh penalties and deportation. The complexities of immigration law are daunting for even experienced legal professionals, making it incredibly difficult for individuals to navigate the system without adequate support. This inequality of access exacerbates existing vulnerabilities, ensuring that non-citizen veterans are disproportionately affected by the inefficiencies and inconsistencies of the system. Furthermore, the narratives highlight the profound psychological toll of navigating this complex and often hostile system. The constant fear of deportation, coupled with the potential for separation from family and community, creates significant stress and anxiety, contributing to mental health challenges that often go unaddressed. This underscores the need for more comprehensive mental health support services specifically tailored to the needs of this vulnerable population.

A comparative analysis of similar cases across different states and even international contexts further reinforces the urgency for change. While the specific regulations and procedures vary, the underlying issues of inter-agency coordination, access to legal resources, and the psychological impact of navigating a complex legal system remain consistent. In some countries, more streamlined and supportive processes are in place to facilitate the integration of non-citizen veterans into society and help them secure citizenship. Examining these best practices provides valuable insights into potential solutions for addressing the systemic failures within the US system. For instance, some countries offer specialized legal assistance programs specifically for military veterans, irrespective of their immigration status, recognizing the unique challenges they face. Others have established clear pathways to citizenship for non-citizen veterans who have served honorably, simplifying the process and minimizing bureaucratic obstacles. This comparative lens emphasizes that the challenges faced by non-citizen veterans are not insurmountable and that alternative, more humane, and practical models exist.

The lack of comprehensive data collection further hinders efforts to understand the true scope of this problem. The absence of reliable and consistent data on the number of non-citizen veterans, their immigration status, and their experiences with the legal system makes it difficult to formulate effective policy responses. This data deficiency hinders the ability to accurately assess the problem's extent and identify specific areas needing improvement. It also prevents the development of targeted interventions and the practical evaluation of existing programs. The need for comprehensive data collection, including longitudinal studies tracking veterans' experiences from recruitment to post-service life is critical for effective policymaking. This data should encompass demographic information, military service records, immigration status, access to legal aid, and mental health outcomes. Such data would provide a comprehensive understanding of the lived experiences of non-citizen veterans, informing the development of effective, evidence-based interventions. The legislative landscape surrounding non-citizen veterans also reveals a pattern of inconsistent and often ineffective efforts. While the Second Chance for Service Act represents a step in the right direction, its scope and impact are limited, leaving many non-citizen veterans without recourse. While commendable in its intent, the act highlights the broader problem of piecemeal legislative approaches that fail to address the underlying systemic failures. True reform requires a comprehensive and coordinated legislative effort, ensuring that all non-citizen veterans are afforded fair and equitable treatment, irrespective of minor infractions or bureaucratic hurdles. Furthermore, this reform should include provisions for retroactive application, ensuring that Those who have already faced deportation or are currently facing deportation proceedings have the opportunity to have their cases reviewed and potentially overturned.

Beyond the immediate legal and bureaucratic challenges, the case studies underscore the profound ethical implications of this situation. The United States is morally obligated to honor the sacrifices made by those who have served in its armed forces, regardless of their immigration status. The implicit promise of citizenship often associated with military service is not just a matter of legal technicality but a deeply rooted societal expectation. Failing to uphold this implicit promise undermines the trust and commitment essential for a functioning society. The deportation of non-citizen veterans sends a deeply unsettling message, undermining the principle of gratitude and reciprocity.

Therefore, addressing this issue is not simply a matter of legal compliance; it demands a fundamental shift in perspective and a recognition of the profound ethical dimensions of the problem. The case studies presented are powerful illustrations of this moral imperative, urging a reassessment of the current system and a commitment to ensuring a just and equitable future for non-citizen veterans.

This requires a multifaceted approach encompassing legislative reform, improved inter-agency coordination, expanded access to legal resources and mental health services, and comprehensive data collection. It also necessitates a broader societal conversation about the moral obligations owed to those who have served their country, regardless of their immigration status. Ultimately, fulfilling the unfulfilled promises made to non-citizen veterans is not just a matter of justice; it reflects the nation's commitment to its values and honoring those who have sacrificed for it. The stories presented in this chapter serve as a stark reminder of the urgency for systemic change and the need for a national commitment to ensuring a more equitable and just future for all who have served. The ongoing struggle of these veterans underscores a critical need for proactive legislation and a fundamental shift in how the nation values and supports those who have defended its interests. Failure to act decisively perpetuates a profound injustice and undermines the very principles upon which the nation stands. The path forward requires legal reforms and a fundamental reassessment of our societal values and commitments.

30 / USING CASE STUDIES TO ADVOCATE FOR CHANGE

The compelling narratives presented in the preceding chapters—the stories of service, sacrifice, and subsequent betrayal—are not merely individual tragedies but potent tools for systemic change. These meticulously documented and ethically anonymized case studies provide concrete evidence of the failures within the current immigration and military systems. They offer more than just anecdotal evidence: they illuminate specific points of failure, revealing the intricate web of bureaucratic obstacles and legal loopholes that trap non-citizen veterans in a cycle of uncertainty and fear. By carefully analyzing these cases, we can identify actionable policy recommendations that directly address one crucial area highlighted by these case studies is the glaring lack of interagency communication and coordination. The military, focused primarily on national security, often fails to adequately inform recruits about the complexities of U.S. immigration law, particularly its impact on those lacking citizenship. This lack of proactive guidance leaves many non-citizen veterans ill-equipped to navigate the legal maze they face post-service. Conversely, immigration authorities frequently lack the crucial context of military service when reviewing cases, leading to a failure to recognize and adequately weigh the unique contributions and sacrifices made by these individuals. This community implementing the case studies also reveals critical shortcomings in access to legal resources. Many non-citizen veterans lack the financial resources or legal expertise to navigate the intricacies of immigration law effectively. The sheer complexity of the legal system and the often unclear nature of procedural requirements create a significant barrier to justice. PFC's inability to secure adequate legal Representation directly contributed to her precarious situation. The case is a stark example of this challenging situation. To address this, policy reforms should prioritize expanded access to pro bono legal services specifically tailored to the needs of non-citizen veterans. This could involve partnerships between legal aid organizations, veteran service groups, and the government to create a more robust and accessible legal support system. Furthermore, creating dedicated legal clinics within military bases and veterans' facilities could ensure that non-citizen veterans receive timely and appropriate assistance.

Another critical area highlighted by the case studies is the inadequacy of mental health services provided to non-citizen veterans. The stress of navigating complex immigration procedures, coupled with the potential threat of deportation, often leads to severe psychological distress. The emotional toll of facing deportation after serving one's country is immense. Many of the veterans suffered heightened levels of anxiety, depression, and PTSD. The failure to provide adequate mental health support not only exacerbates their suffering but also hinders their successful reintegration into civilian life. Policy reforms must prioritize the expansion and improvement of mental health.

The analysis of these case studies also underscores the need for comprehensive data collection. Currently, there is a significant lack of reliable data on the number of non-citizen veterans facing deportation and the specific circumstances surrounding their cases. Without robust data collection, it is impossible to fully understand the scope of the problem, monitor the effectiveness of policy interventions, and advocate for meaningful change. Creating centralized, easily accessible databases tracking non-citizen veteran immigration cases is crucial for evidence-based policy-making. This database should include information on military service records, immigration status, criminal history (if any), legal representation, and outcomes of cases. Such data would provide a clearer picture of these veteran's challenges and allows for identifying patterns and trends, enabling more targeted interventions.

While a positive step, the Second Chance for Service Act is insufficient to address the root causes of this injustice. Its narrow scope and limited applicability leave many non-citizen veterans vulnerable. The case studies reveal a need for more comprehensive and sweeping reforms. This includes streamlining the process for obtaining citizenship for non-citizen veterans, ensuring consistency in applying and enforcing existing immigration laws, and strengthening the protection of non-citizen veterans who have served honorably. It is essential to reform the rules to reflect the unique context of military service better, recognizing the significant contributions and sacrifices made by the international comparisons can also provide valuable insights.

Other nations facing similar challenges have implemented various policies to address the needs of non-citizen veterans.

For instance, some countries offer veterans accelerated citizenship pathways, ensuring their service is recognized and rewarded. Others have established dedicated support services for non-citizen veterans, providing access to comprehensive legal, mental health, and social services. By studying these successful international models, we can identify best practices that can be adapted and implemented in the U.S. context. Comparative research would unveil successful models of interagency coordination and identify effective strategies for addressing the psychological impacts of facing deportation after serving one's country.

Moreover, the need for comprehensive legislative reform extends beyond individual cases. To prevent future injustices, a systemic review of immigration laws and Procedures is imperative. This review should focus on creating a fairer and more humane process that considers non-citizen veterans' unique circumstances and contributions. The emphasis should be on clarity, accessibility, and equity. This includes establishing clear guidelines for assessing the eligibility of non-citizen veterans for citizenship, ensuring due process in deportation proceedings, and providing adequate legal representation and support throughout the process.

Beyond legislative reforms, a broader societal conversation is needed about the moral obligations owed to those who have served their country, regardless of their immigration status. The narratives in this book powerfully remind us of the profound sacrifices made by non-citizen veterans and the nation's moral imperative to uphold its commitments. This conversation must extend beyond legal and policy circles and engage the broader public, fostering a greater understanding of the challenges faced by these individuals and building support for systemic change.

Public awareness campaigns, media outreach, and community engagement is an essential tool in this effort. These campaigns should highlight the human cost of current policies and illustrate the positive impact of providing support and pathways to citizenship for non-citizen veterans.

The case studies provide a powerful impetus for action.

They demand legislative and bureaucratic reforms and a fundamental reassessment of societal values and priorities.

The stories underscore the urgent need for a national commitment to honoring the service and contributions of all those who have defended the nation's interests, regardless of their immigration status. To fail to address the systemic failures highlighted in these cases is not merely a matter of legal compliance; it is a betrayal of the principles of justice, fairness, and gratitude upon which the nation is built. It reflects a nation's failure to honor its promises and uphold its values. The path forward requires not only legal reforms but also a fundamental shift in perspective—one that recognizes the invaluable contributions of non-citizen veterans and prioritizes their well-being and security. Their stories are not merely personal accounts; they are a clarion call for systemic change, a call that cannot be ignored.

Pursuing justice for these veterans is a moral imperative. It is also a testament to the nation's commitment to its values and willingness to honor those who have served and sacrificed for it.

31 / KEY INSIGHTS FROM THE RESEARCH

This book, Unfulfilled Promises, has meticulously documented the plight of non-citizen veterans in the United States, revealing a systemic failure to honor the sacrifices they made in defense of the nation. Our research, encompassing qualitative interviews with deported veterans, an in-depth analysis of legislative and bureaucratic processes, and a comparative study of international immigration policies, unveil a complex web of legal, social, and ethical challenges. The core finding underscores a stark paradox: individuals who risked their lives for the United States are subsequently denied the very citizenship they were implicitly promised, often facing deportation for minor offenses. This injustice is not merely a legal technicality; it carries profound human costs, including family separation, economic hardship, mental health deterioration, and social marginalization.

The legal landscape itself presents formidable obstacles. The complexities of immigration law, coupled with bureaucratic inefficiencies and unequal access to legal representation, often leave noncitizen veterans vulnerable to deportation.

While highlighting a positive legislative attempt, our

analysis of the "Second Chance for Service Act revealed significant limitations in its scope and effectiveness.

Furthermore, the disproportionate impact of minor criminal offenses on deportation outcomes, even in the context of prior military service, underscores a critical flaw in the current system. Many veterans interviewed detailed experiences navigating a system ill-equipped to understand their unique circumstances and contributions. They described feelings of betrayal, abandonment, and profound disillusionment, adding a poignant human dimension to the legal complexities. The stories gathered were not merely anecdotes; they became robust evidence illustrating the human cost of a broken system.

The psychological and social consequences of deportation are equally devastating. The separation from families and communities built in the United States represents an immeasurable loss, often exacerbated by the mental health challenges many veterans already face, such as PTSD. The economic hardship experienced by deported veterans and their families is usually severe, impacting their ability to rebuild their lives in their countries of origin. The reintegration process can be complicated, as they often face social isolation, marginalization, and difficulty accessing crucial support systems. In several cases, veterans reported feeling more alienated and vulnerable in their home countries than they ever did in the United States, a chilling testament to the depth of the damage inflicted by the deportation process. Many described a feeling of being 'twice abandoned' – first by their home countries and then by the government they served.

Our international comparative analysis reveals that other developed nations have implemented more effective and humane policies for non-citizen veterans. These countries offer valuable lessons on integrating military service with immigration status better, emphasizing the need for more proactive and compassionate approaches. The contrast between the US system and the more supportive systems in other nations reinforces the urgency for comprehensive reform. Analyzing the successful international models—which include streamlined pathways to citizenship, increased access to legal aid, and more robust support systems for reintegration—highlighted the possibility of a more just and equitable approach. The comparison was not merely academic; it provided a blueprint for positive change, demonstrating that effective and humane solutions are achievable.

The detailed case studies presented throughout the book illustrate these broader systemic failures. Each case examined provides unique insights into the individual struggles faced by non-citizen veterans and the bureaucratic hurdles they encountered. These narratives are crucial in humanizing the abstract data and legal complexities, giving a voice to the often-overlooked experiences of these individuals. One case, for example, highlighted the devastating impact of a minor traffic violation on a veteran with an exemplary military record, resulting in immediate deportation without proper consideration of his service or contributions. Another case study showed a veteran's tireless efforts to appeal their deportation order, navigating a complex legal system with limited resources and support, eventually finding a measure of success through the intervention of a dedicated advocacy group. However, the success in this second case was not typical, highlighting the systemic issues of inconsistent application of laws and policies. These detailed narratives provided crucial evidence, underpinning the overall argument for systemic change.

This research underscores a crucial moral imperative: upholding the nation's commitment to its veterans, regardless of their citizenship status. The ethical implications of deporting individuals who have risked their lives in service to the country are profound and cannot be ignored. The United States ensures that all veterans, regardless of origin, receive the support and recognition they deserve. This responsibility extends beyond mere legal compliance; it demands a fundamental shift in how society values and protects its defenders. The notion that military service should automatically translate to citizenship is worth revisiting and refining. Our research demonstrates how the current system falls short of this ideal and provides compelling evidence for reform.

I'm looking forward to several areas that need to be looked at. Future research should focus on developing more nuanced measures to assess the long-term impact of deportation on veterans' mental and physical health. I want to explore the effigies.

In conclusion, Unfulfilled Promises calls for a fundamental shift in how the United States treats its non-citizen veterans. The findings that were presented would need immediate and comprehensive action. A more just and equitable immigration system is not merely a matter of legal compliance but a moral obligation. This requires a concerted effort from policymakers, advocacy groups, and the public to address the systemic failures highlighted in this study.

Ultimately, honoring the sacrifices of non-citizen veterans is not merely a matter of justice; it affirms the nation's values and is a testament to its commitment to upholding its promises. The need for systemic change is not just urgent; it is a moral imperative. The stories, data, and comparative analyses presented in this book provide a robust case for meaningful reform, ensuring that the sacrifices of non-citizen veterans are finally recognized and honored. The ultimate goal is a system that reflects the values of gratitude, justice, and compassion.

32 / HONORING THE CONTRIBUTIONS OF NONCITIZEN VETERANS

The preceding chapters have laid bare the systemic injustices faced by non-citizen veterans in the United States. We have documented the bureaucratic hurdles, the legal loopholes exploited to justify deportation, and the devastating human consequences of this national failure to uphold its commitments. However, the problem extends beyond the legal and bureaucratic realms; it resides in a deeply ingrained societal narrative that undervalues the contributions of these individuals and fails to acknowledge their profound sacrifices. Reframing this narrative is crucial to achieving meaningful and lasting systemic change. The current discourse often frames immigration through a lens of security and national threat, overshadowing the contributions of individuals who have demonstrably risked their lives for this nation. This perspective ignores the crucial reality that these veterans, through their service, have embodied the ideals of patriotism and sacrifice often cited as the cornerstones of American identity.

To truly honor these veterans, we must actively challenge this limited narrative. Acknowledging their service is not enough; we must also actively work to integrate their stories into the broader American narrative of patriotism and sacrifice.

This requires a multi-pronged approach encompassing educational initiatives, public awareness campaigns, and a fundamental shift in how immigration and military service are discussed. Our educational systems, from primary schools to universities, need to incorporate the stories of non-citizen veterans into their curricula. This isn't about adding another "feel-good" story; it's about providing a more complete and nuanced understanding of American history and the diverse contributions that have shaped the nation. Including these narratives will foster empathy and understanding, challenging the existing stereotypes and prejudice surrounding immigration.

Furthermore, public awareness campaigns are vital in shifting public perception. These campaigns should go beyond simple announcements and slogans. They should utilize compelling storytelling, sharing the personal accounts of veterans who have been deported or face the threat of deportation. These stories can humanize the issue, making it relatable and understandable to a broader audience. The aim is to raise awareness and foster emotional engagement, compelling individuals to actively support policy reforms that protect these veterans. The power of personal narratives cannot be overstated. Through carefully crafted documentaries, podcasts, and other media formats, we can connect with the public on a visceral level, compelling them to demand justice and accountability.

The challenge is to move beyond abstract discussions of legal technicalities and focus on the human cost of these policies. The stories of families torn apart, careers shattered, and lives upended serve as powerful testimonies to the urgent need for reform. These are not simply statistics; they are individuals who answered the nation's call to arms, only to be betrayed by the very system they served. Their stories offer a powerful counter-narrative to the often-simplistic and dehumanizing rhetoric surrounding immigration. The comparative analysis presented earlier in this book highlights the stark contrast between the U.S. approach and the policies adopted by other nations. Many countries offer pathways to citizenship for foreign nationals who serve in their militaries. These examples demonstrate that it is not inherently impossible or impractical to create a system that honors the contributions of non-citizen veterans. By studying these alternative approaches, we can identify best practices and adapt them to the specific circumstances of the United States. This comparative lens underscores the fact that the U.S. system is not simply flawed; it is an outlier, failing to align with the practices of many other developed nations that value the contributions of their foreign-born service members. While presenting significant challenges, the legislative landscape also offers opportunities for positive change.

While imperfect, the "Second Chance for Service Act" represents a step in the right direction. However, its success depends on broader societal support and a sustained commitment to reform. This requires advocacy from veterans' organizations, legal groups, and human rights activists. It also demands a concerted effort from lawmakers to prioritize the well-being of non-citizen veterans over political expediency. The act serves as a crucial framework; however, its effectiveness hinges on proactive implementation and a robust system for identifying and assisting eligible veterans. The challenges of navigating the complex bureaucratic procedures inherent in the act remain a significant obstacle for many veterans. Further legislative action might be required to streamline the application process, ensuring all eligible veterans can access its provisions effectively.

Beyond legislation, the judiciary's role is paramount. Judges can interpret the law in a way that prioritizes fairness and equity. They can challenge the narrow interpretations that often lead to the deportation of non-citizen veterans. This demands a judiciary that is both informed and sensitive to the nuances of military service and the complex implications of immigration law. The judiciary's interpretation of existing legislation can significantly shape the lives of non-citizens and veterans, emphasizing the importance of legal challenges to unjust deportations.

Furthermore, the role of media in shaping public opinion cannot be overstated. Responsible journalism that accurately and compassionately reports on the stories of non-citizen veterans can significantly shift public discourse. Journalists can hold the government accountable and ensure transparency in the immigration process. By providing a platform for the voices of these veterans and their families, the media can amplify their experiences and push for systemic change. Avoiding sensationalized or biased reporting is critical, ensuring that the focus remains on the human stories and the underlying systemic issues.

Finally, the responsibility to honor these veterans rests with government institutions, advocacy groups, and the broader American public. Every citizen has a role in ensuring that these individuals are treated with the dignity, respect, and gratitude they deserve. We can create a more just and equitable society by demanding accountability from our elected officials, supporting veterans' organizations, and actively challenging the narratives that marginalize these individuals. This is not merely a matter of legal compliance; it is a moral imperative, reflecting the values of compassion, gratitude, and justice that should underpin our national identity. The path forward requires sustained engagement, a willingness to challenge existing power structures, and an unwavering commitment to honoring the sacrifices of those who have served this nation. Only then can we truly begin to fulfill the unfulfilled promises made to these brave individuals. The task ahead demands a fundamental reassessment of our values and a sincere commitment to building a society that genuinely honors its heroes. Failing to act decisively leaves a stain on the nation's conscience and perpetuates an injustice that cries out for redress.

33 / UNANSWERED QUESTIONS AND FURTHER INQUIRY

The preceding chapters have detailed the systemic failures that led to the deportation of non-citizen veterans, highlighting the legal, bureaucratic, and human costs of this injustice. However, numerous critical questions remain unanswered, demanding further research to understand the scope and depth of this problem entirely and to inform more effective solutions. This section outlines key areas for future inquiry, offering a roadmap for scholars, policymakers, and advocates striving for meaningful change.

Firstly, a more comprehensive investigation into the psychological and societal impacts of deportation on non-citizen veterans is crucial. While this book has touched upon the trauma and alienation experienced by these individuals, more in-depth qualitative research is needed. This research should employ in-depth interviews, focus groups, and ethnographic studies to capture the lived experiences of deported veterans and their families. Such studies should explore the long-term effects of deportation on mental health, family dynamics, and social integration in their countries of origin or resettlement locations. The research should also analyze the specific challenges faced by veterans with disabilities or pre-existing mental health conditions, as they are likely to face even more significant difficulties adjusting to life outside the United States after deportation. Further research should also explore the impact on veterans' families who may remain in the U.S., separated from their loved ones through deportation. This includes analyzing the economic consequences for families, the emotional toll on children, and the challenges of maintaining transnational relationships.

Secondly, a closer examination of the role of prosecutorial discretion in deportation cases is essential. While the law may prescribe specific outcomes, the decisions of individual prosecutors significantly influence the fate of non-citizen veterans. Further research should analyze the factors that influence prosecutorial decisions, investigating whether implicit biases, resource constraints, or other systemic factors contribute to disproportionately harsh outcomes for this population. This research could involve analyzing a large dataset of deportation cases and employing statistical methods to identify patterns and correlations. It could also include interviews with prosecutors to understand their perspectives and decision-making processes. A qualitative analysis of case files could also provide valuable insights into the nuances of each case, revealing potential systemic biases in how these cases are handled. The study should also explore whether prosecutorial training adequately addresses the unique circumstances of non-citizen veterans and the ethical implications of deporting individuals who have served the nation.

Thirdly, comparative studies with countries that have similar populations of non-citizen veterans could offer valuable insights and potential solutions. Research should explore how different nations address the citizenship and immigration status of veterans who served in their armed forces, mainly focusing on those who may have served in situations with less-than-perfect legal standing. This could involve analyzing other countries' laws, policies, and procedures, comparing their effectiveness, and identifying best practices. Cross-national comparisons could offer valuable lessons that could inform policy reforms in the United States. This could involve analyzing the legal frameworks of other nations, studying the experiences of non-citizen veterans in those countries, and conducting comparative case studies. This research should also explore the cultural and political contexts that shape immigration policies in different countries and how these contexts influence the treatment of non-citizen veterans. The focus here should be on identifying successful strategies for integrating non-citizen veterans into society and ensuring they receive the recognition and benefits they deserve.

Fourthly, it is crucial to study advocacy efforts and their effectiveness in promoting legislative change. This includes analyzing the successes and challenges veterans' organizations, legal aid groups, and other advocacy groups working on behalf of non-citizen veterans face. The study should investigate the strategies used by these groups, the political and social contexts that shape their actions, and the impact of their advocacy efforts on legislative outcomes.

This could involve analyzing publicly available data on legislation, interviewing advocacy group leaders and staff, and examining the media coverage of these advocacy campaigns. The research should also explore the role of public opinion and social movements in shaping the debate surrounding immigration and veterans' rights. A deeper understanding of effective advocacy strategies will inform future efforts to improve the treatment of noncitizen veterans.

Fifthly, a significant area for future research lies in exploring the long-term consequences of the current policies.

While this book has highlighted the immediate impacts of deportation, longitudinal studies are needed to understand the long-term effects on deported veterans, their families, and the broader community. Such studies should track the well-being of deported veterans over time, monitoring their economic conditions, mental health, and social integration in their new environments. Longitudinal studies can provide a comprehensive picture of the lasting consequences of deportation and reveal important information about the effectiveness of various interventions. This requires establishing robust data collection methods and ensuring long-term ethical compliance in data management and research subject consent.

Sixthly, examining the intersection of race and ethnicity in deportation cases is crucial. Research should investigate whether racial and ethnic biases play a role in the decisions to deport non-citizen veterans. This could involve quantitative and qualitative analyses of deportation data, exploring whether certain racial or ethnic groups are disproportionately affected. The research should also examine the experiences of non-citizen veterans from different racial and ethnic backgrounds, documenting their specific challenges and how they intersect with their immigration status. This analysis would require a sensitive approach, using qualitative methods to understand the narratives of affected individuals and examining existing data to discern potential systemic biases. The research must be meticulous to avoid perpetuating stereotypes and ensure an accurate representation of the experiences of each group.

Furthermore, the effectiveness of legislative interventions such as the Second Chance for Service Act needs closer scrutiny. While such acts represent significant steps toward addressing the issue, future research should examine their actual impact on the ground. This involves assessing the number of veterans who have successfully utilized the provisions of the act, identifying any obstacles encountered in accessing these provisions, and measuring the extent to which the act has improved the lives of non-citizen veterans.

Analyzing this effectiveness requires tracking the success rate of applications and assessing the changes in deportation rates for veterans after the act's implementation. Further, this research could explore potential avenues for legislative improvements to broaden the scope and effectiveness of the Act, making it easier for non-citizen veterans to benefit from its provisions.

Finally, the role of public awareness and education in influencing policy change needs to be investigated. This includes studying how public perception of non-citizen veterans shapes political discourse and policy decisions. This research could involve surveys and focus groups to understand public attitudes toward non-citizen veterans and their deportation. It could also analyze media representations of non-citizen veterans to know how they are portrayed in public discourse. This understanding will inform strategies to raise public awareness and build support for policy reforms. Moreover, exploring innovative public education and engagement methods, such as social media campaigns and community outreach programs, is essential to fostering greater understanding and support for non-citizen veterans' rights. By understanding the nuances of public perceptions, more effective advocacy strategies can be developed to address public misconceptions and garner public support for necessary changes.

In conclusion, while this book has provided a critical analysis of the plight of non-citizen veterans, numerous questions remain open and demand further research. By undertaking the studies suggested above, we can gain a more profound understanding of this complex issue, leading to more informed policy decisions and ultimately achieving a more just and equitable system that upholds its commitments to those who have served the nation. The future of these veterans and a just society depends on our willingness to confront these unanswered questions and work toward meaningful, lasting solutions. The ethical imperative demands nothing less.

34 / UPHOLDING THE NATION'S COMMITMENT TO ITS VETERANS

The preceding chapters have laid bare the stark realities faced by non-citizen veterans in the United States: the bureaucratic labyrinth they navigate, the legal loopholes exploited against them, and the profound human cost of deportation. We have examined the legislative landscape, the inconsistencies in the application, and the devastating impact on individuals who risked life and limb for their adopted country, only to be cast aside upon minor infractions. But beyond the legal arguments and statistical analyses lies a fundamental moral imperative that demands our urgent attention: the nation's unwavering ethical obligation to its veterans, regardless of their citizenship status.

This obligation transcends legal technicalities and bureaucratic procedures. It is rooted in a profound sense of gratitude, respect, and justice. These individuals answered the nation's call to arms, embodying the highest ideals of service, courage, and sacrifice. They volunteered to defend the very principles upon which this nation is founded –freedom, liberty, and the pursuit of happiness. To then cast them adrift, vulnerable to deportation for relatively minor offenses after their service, is a profound betrayal of the trust they placed in this nation and a stark repudiation of the values it claims to uphold.

The ethical framework underpinning this obligation rests on several pillars. First, there's the principle of reciprocity. These veterans offered their loyalty, skills, and, often, their very lives in defense of the nation. In return, they were promised opportunities, security, and a chance to build a future within the society they defended. To deny them this, to strip them of their hard-earned standing and promise them a future is a fundamental breach of the implied contract between the nation and its defenders. This is not merely a matter of legal rights but of basic fairness and moral decency.

Secondly, there is the compelling argument of gratitude. These men and women risked their well-being for the collective good. They endured hardship, trauma, and, often, profound loss. Their service contributed to the safety and security enjoyed by all citizens, regardless of their background. It is morally unconscionable to repay such sacrifice with abandonment and indifference, particularly when minor infractions become the pretext for deportation.

The nation's gratitude should manifest in words of appreciation and tangible actions that reflect a genuine commitment to its well-being.

Thirdly, and perhaps most importantly, is the principle of justice. Justice demands that we treat individuals fairly and equitably, based on their merits and actions, not on arbitrary factors like their citizenship status. To prioritize bureaucratic efficiency or narrow legal interpretations over the profound human cost of deportation is a travesty of justice. It is a betrayal of the ideals of equality and fairness that this nation claims to champion. The focus should be on the individual's contributions, character, and commitment to the country rather than technicalities that obscure the fundamental injustice.

The moral imperative extends beyond individual cases. It requires a systemic reevaluation of how we treat non-citizen veterans, demanding a profound shift in our national conscience and our legal framework. This necessitates a robust review of existing immigration policies, identifying and dismantling those provisions that disproportionately impact this vulnerable population. We need to examine the fairness and consistency of existing laws, ensuring that the same standards of justice are applied to all veterans, regardless of their immigration status.

The issue is not merely about amending laws but about changing hearts and minds. It demands a broader societal conversation about our values and responsibilities towards those who have served our nation. We need to challenge the narrative that frames veterans who are not citizens as somehow less deserving of our respect and compassion. We must actively engage with the diverse communities that make up our nation, ensuring that the voices of non-citizen veterans are heard and amplified and their experiences understood and acknowledged.

This ethical obligation also entails providing adequate support and resources for these veterans and their families. Many face significant challenges upon return from service, including PTSD, physical injuries, and difficulty reintegrating into civilian life. These challenges are often compounded by the threat of deportation, further exacerbating their distress. Providing comprehensive mental health services, vocational training, and legal assistance is not simply an act of charity; it is a moral imperative stemming from our debt to those who have served.

Furthermore, providing legal representation to those facing deportation is a crucial step in ensuring they receive a fair hearing and have the opportunity to present their case fully.

The call for systemic change and ethical responsibility is

not merely a plea for compassion but a demand for justice and a recognition of our nation's fundamental moral obligations. It requires a multifaceted approach, encompassing legislative reforms, bureaucratic overhauls, and a fundamental shift in societal attitudes. It demands a commitment to transparency, accountability, and fairness in treating those who have risked everything for this nation. Failing to act decisively to address this injustice with the urgency it demands is a moral failing and a fundamental betrayal of the principles upon which this nation was founded. It is a disservice to those who served and a stain on our national character.

We have seen examples of legislative attempts, such as the Second Chance for Service Act, aiming to address this issue. However, these efforts often fall short, highlighting the need for more comprehensive and effective legislation. A more robust framework is required that protects non-citizen veterans from deportation for minor offenses and offers a clear pathway to citizenship for those who have demonstrably served the nation with honor and distinction.

This framework should be built upon principles of justice, fairness, and gratitude, ensuring that the sacrifices of these veterans are not disregarded.

The international landscape also offers valuable insights. Many nations provide pathways to citizenship for those who serve in their militaries, recognizing the profound sacrifices made and the enduring commitment demonstrated. By examining these successful models, we can identify best practices and adapt them to the specific context of the United States, strengthening our existing framework and establishing a more humane and just system. This comparative analysis will unveil potential legislative solutions and inspire a more comprehensive policy response addressing the socio-economic and psychological ramifications experienced by these veterans and their families.

Ultimately, the moral imperative of upholding the nation's commitment to its veterans transcends legal debates and political posturing. It is a matter of fundamental human decency, a testament to our values, and a reflection of our national character. By acknowledging and addressing the injustice faced by non-citizen veterans, we can reaffirm our commitment to justice, fairness, and gratitude, strengthening the bonds that unite our nation and honoring the profound sacrifices made by those who have served. Failure to do so constitutes a profound moral failure with long-lasting and far-reaching consequences. The path forward demands legislative action and a fundamental change in our societal attitudes toward those who have defended this nation, regardless of their origin. The future of these veterans and, indeed, the moral fabric of this nation rests on our willingness to embrace this crucial responsibility. The ethical imperative demands nothing less than a complete overhaul of the system and a profound commitment to justice for all who have served.

35 / TOWARDS A MORE JUST AND EQUITABLE IMMIGRATION SYSTEM

The preceding chapters have illuminated the profound injustices faced by non-citizen veterans in the United States. We've delved into the complex interplay of military service, immigration law, and bureaucratic processes, revealing a system rife with inconsistencies, loopholes, and a fundamental lack of empathy for those who have risked their lives to defend this nation. The stories shared, the data analyzed, and the examined legal precedents converge on a single, undeniable conclusion: the current system is broken, and its failures inflict profound and lasting harm on individuals who deserve far better.

To merely acknowledge the problem, however, is insufficient. The urgency of the situation demands concrete action, a decisive shift towards a more just and equitable immigration system that prioritizes the well-being of non-citizen veterans. This necessitates a multi-pronged approach, addressing legislative shortcomings, reforming bureaucratic processes, and fostering a cultural shift in how we perceive and value the contributions of these individuals.

One of the most critical areas for reform lies in the legislative arena. While efforts like the Second Chance for Service

Act represent a step in the right direction, they are far from comprehensive. Current laws often prioritize punitive measures over compassionate consideration, leading to the deportation of individuals who have served honorably, often for minor offenses that would not lead to similar consequences for citizens. A comprehensive overhaul is required, one that explicitly addresses the unique circumstances of non-citizen veterans and prioritizes their integration and well-being within American society. This includes streamlining the naturalization process for veterans and ensuring their military service is given significantly weight in any immigration proceedings. A presumption of good faith and a recognition of their service to the nation should be enshrined in law, shifting the burden of proof away from the veteran and onto the government to demonstrate compelling reasons for deportation.

Furthermore, the bureaucratic hurdles faced by non-citizen veterans must be dismantled. The labyrinthine nature of immigration processes, often characterized by delays, inconsistencies, and a lack of transparency only exacerbate the trauma and uncertainty these individuals endure. Streamlining these processes, ensuring clear communication, and providing dedicated support services tailored to non-citizen veterans' needs are crucial steps toward achieving a more just and equitable system. This could involve the creation of a specialized unit within the Department of Homeland Security or establishing a dedicated legal aid program to assist veterans in navigating the complexities of immigration law. The goal should be to reduce bureaucratic obstacles and ensure a fair and efficient process that recognizes the unique contributions of those who have served.

Beyond legislative and bureaucratic reforms, a fundamental shift in societal attitudes is necessary. The pervasive Misconceptions and prejudices surrounding immigration often lead to the marginalization and demonization of non-citizen veterans, further compounding their suffering. Public awareness campaigns to educate the public about the contributions of non-citizen veterans and the injustices they face are crucial in fostering a more inclusive and supportive environment. Sharing their stories, amplifying their voices, and highlighting the ethical implications of their mistreatment can help challenge existing biases and promote a greater understanding of their unique circumstances. This could involve partnerships with veteran organizations, community leaders, and media outlets to disseminate information and foster a national conversation.

International comparisons can also offer valuable insights into best practices. Many other countries have established more robust and compassionate systems for integrating non-citizen veterans into their societies, offering valuable lessons for the United States. By studying these models, we can identify successful strategies for streamlining processes, ensuring due process, and fostering a more supportive environment for those who have served. This comparative analysis can inform policy recommendations and provide a framework for systemic change. Such analysis should include an examination of the legislative frameworks, bureaucratic procedures, and societal attitudes toward non-citizen veterans in countries with more successful integration programs. This might involve conducting case studies of specific countries and analyzing their legislative and policy approaches.

The pursuit of a more just and equitable immigration system for non-citizen veterans demands a holistic and sustained effort. It requires legislative action, bureaucratic reform, and a fundamental change in societal attitudes. Creating a National commission addressing this issue could provide a framework for ongoing dialogue and stakeholders collaboration. This commission could bring together experts in immigration law, military affairs, social work, and other relevant fields to develop comprehensive recommendations for policy reform and public awareness campaigns. The commission's work could also involve regular consultations with non-citizen veterans, ensuring their voices and experiences are central to the process.

Furthermore, the investment in comprehensive research is crucial. This includes longitudinal studies tracking the experiences of non-citizen veterans throughout the research should examine the immigration process, analyze the effectiveness of different policy interventions, and assess the long-term impacts of deportation on individuals and communities. It should inform evidence-based policymaking and ensure that any reforms are grounded in thoroughly understanding the issue's complexities. The data gathered could also be used to advocate for more effective legal protections and support services for non-citizen veterans. Furthermore, the research should explore the economic and social costs associated with the deportation of non-citizen veterans, highlighting the broader societal implications of this issue.

Finally, the moral imperative demands that we not only address the injustices faced by non-citizen veterans but also prevent future occurrences. This requires ongoing vigilance, a commitment to transparency and accountability, and a system that prioritizes the well-being of individuals over bureaucratic efficiency or political expediency. A system that values the contributions of all who serve, regardless of their citizenship status, is not just a matter of justice but also a reflection of our national values and a testament to our commitment to a perfect union. The path forward is clear: a commitment to systemic change, a dedication to ethical responsibility, and an unwavering resolve to honor the sacrifices made by those who have defended our nation.

Failing to act decisively is a failure of our legal system and collective conscience. The future of these veterans and the integrity of our nation depend on our commitment to fulfilling the promises made to those who have served with unwavering courage and dedication. The nation's honor is at stake.

ACKNOWLEDGMENTS

This book would not have been possible without the support and contributions of numerous individuals. First and foremost, I extend my deepest gratitude to the non-citizen veterans who bravely shared their personal stories and experiences. Their courage, resilience, and willingness to participate in this research are the heart of this book. I sincerely appreciate their vulnerability in sharing their often traumatic experiences.

My sincere thanks also go to the legal professionals, advocates, and researchers who generously provided their expertise and insights. Their guidance and support were invaluable in navigating the complexities of immigration law and military affairs. Specific thanks are due to Dr. Gonzales of Cal State Dominguez Hills. I sincerely thank my family and friends for their unwavering patience and support throughout the writing process. Their encouragement and understanding were instrumental in my success.

BIBLIOGRAPHY

REFERENCES:

1. AMERICAN EXILE on Vimeo. (n.d.).
    - Vimeo
    - Retrieved February 8, 2024, from
    - https://vimeo.com/483328487
2. Deportation of non-citizen military veterans: A critical analysis of implications. (n.d.).
    - EBSCOhost
    - Retrieved February 8, 2024, from
    - https://web.p.ebscohost.com/ehost/pdfviewer/pdfviewer?vid=2&sid=2823dbb3-bf2d-43f2-b0d9-109598f8c127%40redis
3. Deported veterans are not entitled to the health care they deserve. (n.d.).
    - ProQuest
    - Retrieved February 8, 2024, from
    - https://www.proquest.com/docview/2618198085?pq-origsite=primo&parentSession-Id=k%2F0%2F5yZym3feWD 5wUX0dPhEMlMfb4T8X-Id76A18sFi0%3D&sourcetype=Tr ade%20Journals
4. Deported veterans, stranded far from home after years of military service, press Biden to bring them back. (n.d.).
    - Gale In Context: Opposing Viewpoints
    - Retrieved February 8, 2024, from
    - p=OVIC&u=csudh&id=GALE%7CJOHD-IF281918221&v= 2.1&it=r&sid=Primo&aty=ip
5. House passes bill to bring back deported veterans. (n.d.).
    - Gale General OneFile
    - Retrieved February 8, 2024, from
    - https://go.gale.com/ps/i.do?p=ITOF&u=csudh&id=GALE%7CA729730737&v=2.1&it=r&sid=bookmark-ITOF&asid=ee2f0001
6. ProQuest Ebook Central—Reader. (n.d.).
    - ProQuest

- Retrieved February 8, 2024, from
- https://ebookcentral.proquest.com/lib/csudh/reader.action?docID=29703709

7. Military pathways to United States citizenship: Latina/o "aliens and non-citizen nationals" and military service. (n.d.).
   - ProQuest
   - Retrieved February 8, 2024, from
   - https://www.proquest.com/docview/1694063969?accountid=10347&pq-origsite=primo&parentSession-Id=zp8rAZNY2fOFHi1475Rn um%2B4IDPdpOBt88VyhMkl-Miw%3D&sourcetype=Schol arly%20Journals
8. Chairman Takano, Representatives Vargas, and Grijalva have introduced a comprehensive legislative effort to prevent the deportation of military veterans in the United States. (n.d.). Gale In Context: Opposing Viewpoints
   - Retrieved February 8, 2024, from
   - p=OVIC&u=csudh&v=2.1&it=r&id=GALE%7CA652676156&retrievalId=64af6242-e4f6-42e9-a2fd-55a643a8e330&inPS=true&linkSource=inter-link&sid=book mark-OVIC
9. The story of America's deported veterans remains largely untold. (n.d.).
   - Gale Academic OneFile
   - Retrieved February 8, 2024, from
   - p=AONE&u=csudh&id=GALE%7CA499720112&v=2.1&it =r
10. USC 1440: Naturalization through active-duty service in the Armed Forces during World War I, World War II, Korean hostilities, Vietnam hostilities, or other periods of military hostilities. (n.d.).
    - Retrieved from
    - https://uscode.house.gov/view.xhtml?req=granuleid%3AUSC-prelim-title8-section1440&num=0&edition=prelim
11. DOD addresses recruiting shortfall challenges.(n.d.).
    - U.S. Department of Defense
    - Retrieved from
    - https://www.defense.gov/News/News-Stories/Article/article/3616786/dod-addresses-recruiting-shortfall-challenges/#:~:text=A%20smaller%20eligi-

ble%20populatio
n.,decreases%20the%20propensity%20to%20serve

AUTHOR BIOGRAPHY

Louis Raprager III is a veteran of the U.S. Navy and advocates for specializing in veteran outreach. Their research focuses on the intersection of these fields, with a particular interest in the experiences of marginalized groups within the military and immigration systems. He holds a Business Administration and Human Resources Management degree from California State University Dominguez Hills. He has conducted extensive qualitative research, including numerous interviews with non-citizen veterans, and possesses a strong analytical ability to interpret legislative and bureaucratic processes. Louis Raprager III has also published multiple articles in peer-reviewed journals and is the author of Navigating the Waves of Change: A Veterans Journey. Their work seeks to bridge the gap between academic analysis and public understanding of complex social issues.

www.ingramcontent.com/pod-product-compliance
Lightning Source LLC
LaVergne TN
LVHW010547160826
845677LV00013B/3035

* 9 7 9 8 8 9 6 9 1 2 6 7 5 *